GOLD VS THE INDIAN STOCK MARKET

HISTORY AND THE WAY FORWARD

SHAGUN JAIN

Copyright © Shagun Jain
All Rights Reserved.

This book has been self-published with all reasonable efforts taken to make the material error-free by the author. No part of this book shall be used, reproduced in any manner whatsoever without written permission from the author, except in the case of brief quotations embodied in critical articles and reviews.

The Author of this book is solely responsible and liable for its content including but not limited to the views, representations, descriptions, statements, information, opinions and references ["Content"]. The Content of this book shall not constitute or be construed or deemed to reflect the opinion or expression of the Publisher or Editor. Neither the Publisher nor Editor endorse or approve the Content of this book or guarantee the reliability, accuracy or completeness of the Content published herein and do not make any representations or warranties of any kind, express or implied, including but not limited to the implied warranties of merchantability, fitness for a particular purpose. The Publisher and Editor shall not be liable whatsoever for any errors, omissions, whether such errors or omissions result from negligence, accident, or any other cause or claims for loss or damages of any kind, including without limitation, indirect or consequential loss or damage arising out of use, inability to use, or about the reliability, accuracy or sufficiency of the information contained in this book.

Made with ♥ on the Notion Press Platform
www.notionpress.com

Contents

Foreword v

Acknowledgements vii

Purpose of the Book ix

Who Should Read This Book xi

How to Use This Book for Investment Decisions xiii

Historical Context And Evolution

   1. Gold As An Investment In India   3

   2. The Evolution Of The Indian Stock Market   10

   3. The Relationship Between Gold And The Stock Market   19

Analysis Of Gold Vs. Stock Market Investments

   4. Risk And Volatility Analysis   29

   5. Gold As A Hedge Against Inflation And Currency Fluctuations   36

   6. Macroeconomic And Political Influences   43

Strategic Investment Approaches

   7. Portfolio Diversification Strategies   57

   8. Choosing Between Gold And Stocks: Key Considerations   69

   9. Technological Impact On Investments In Gold And Stocks   81

The Way Forward

   10. Future Outlook For Gold And Indian Equities   95

   11. Building A Balanced Investment Portfolio   105

Contents

Conclusion

Appendices 127

References 131

Foreword

In today's fast-evolving financial landscape, investing has become more complex than ever, especially in a country like India, where economic growth, cultural traditions, and global influences converge to shape the investment ecosystem. Indian investors are uniquely positioned, balancing the ancient, time-tested appeal of gold with the modern potential of the stock market. Gold vs. The Indian Stock Market: History and the Way Forward is an insightful exploration into these two pivotal asset classes, offering readers a strategic guide on how to build a resilient, well-rounded portfolio in the face of market volatility and economic uncertainty.

This book couldn't be more timely. With inflationary pressures, currency fluctuations, and global uncertainties affecting India's economy, it's essential for investors to have a deep understanding of the tools at their disposal. Gold, with its reputation as a safe-haven asset, has provided security across generations, particularly in times of financial turmoil. Conversely, equities represent growth, innovation, and wealth creation, capturing the promise of India's thriving sectors like technology, finance, and consumer goods. Together, these assets provide a powerful combination that can help investors weather economic cycles and capitalize on opportunities for growth.

What sets this book apart is its accessibility. The author distills complex economic and financial concepts into practical, actionable insights suitable for both new investors and seasoned professionals. From the historical significance of gold in Indian culture to the dynamic nature of modern equity markets, each section of the book offers clarity and strategic guidance. The book also addresses emerging trends and technological innovations—such as digital gold, robo-advisors, and algorithmic trading—that are reshaping how we approach investing today. For those looking to balance tradition with modernity, or seeking a framework to navigate India's unique economic environment, this book serves as an invaluable resource.

Gold vs. The Indian Stock Market: History and the Way Forward is more than just an investment guide; it's a roadmap for building wealth and preserving financial security in an uncertain world. Whether you are at the beginning of your investment journey or looking to refine your approach with advanced strategies, this book will empower you with knowledge, confidence, and a long-term perspective.

Acknowledgements

Writing Gold vs. The Indian Stock Market: History and the Way Forward has been a journey of learning, reflection, and discovery, and it would not have been possible without the support and guidance of many individuals who contributed to its creation.

First and foremost, I extend my deepest gratitude to my family for their unwavering encouragement and belief in me throughout this endeavor. Their patience, understanding, and constant support gave me the strength to bring this book to life.

I am also profoundly thankful to the many mentors, financial advisors, and economic experts who generously shared their insights, helping me to refine the concepts and strategies presented in this book. Their expertise and perspectives on the intricacies of India's financial landscape have been invaluable.

To my friends and colleagues in the financial community, thank you for engaging in countless discussions that sparked new ideas and deepened my understanding of the complexities surrounding gold and equity investments. Your insights and real-world experiences have enriched this work in immeasurable ways.

Finally, I am deeply grateful to you, the reader. Whether you are a seasoned investor or just beginning your financial journey, your desire to learn and grow is the ultimate motivation behind this book. It is my sincere hope that this work serves as a valuable resource, helping you make informed decisions and empowering you to navigate India's dynamic economic landscape with confidence.

ACKNOWLEDGEMENTS

Thank you all for being part of this journey.

Purpose Of The Book

The purpose of this book, Gold vs. The Indian Stock Market: History and the Way Forward, is to offer investors a comprehensive understanding of two pivotal asset classes—gold and equities—and how they can be strategically combined to build resilient, long-term wealth. In a country with deep-rooted cultural connections to gold and an emerging economic powerhouse in the global markets, Indian investors face unique opportunities and challenges in wealth management. This book aims to guide readers through the historical performance, economic significance, and future potential of both gold and equities, helping them navigate their distinct roles in portfolio diversification.

By examining the evolving dynamics of the Indian economy, this book seeks to equip readers with practical insights into asset allocation, risk management, and investment strategies that align with various financial goals and market conditions. From understanding the stabilizing power of gold during periods of economic uncertainty to leveraging equities for capital appreciation during growth phases, readers will gain the knowledge needed to make informed decisions in both favorable and volatile environments. This book also explores emerging trends and technological advancements in the investment landscape, such as digital gold, robo-advisors, and blockchain, which are reshaping access to and management of these assets.

Through historical data, case studies, and future forecasts, this book provides a well-rounded perspective that empowers readers to adopt a balanced, adaptable approach to investing. Gold vs. The Indian Stock Market: History and the Way Forward is designed to be an essential resource for Indian investors, both new and experienced, who are looking to build a portfolio that is growth-oriented, resilient, and tailored to the unique dynamics of India's economic landscape.

Who Should Read This Book

Gold vs. The Indian Stock Market: History and the Way Forward is ideal for a diverse range of readers:

New Investors: Provides foundational knowledge on gold and equities, covering essential concepts like asset allocation and risk management.

Experienced Investors: Offers advanced strategies like dynamic asset allocation, exploring both traditional and tech-enabled approaches.

Indian Investors with Cultural Affinity for Gold: Guides readers on viewing gold as both a cultural asset and a strategic investment.

Ethical Investors: Highlights sustainable investment options, including ESG considerations within gold and equity portfolios.

Financial Advisors: Acts as a resource for professionals advising clients on balanced, resilient portfolios.

Tech-Savvy Investors: Explores digital gold, robo-advisors, and online trading platforms, aligning with modern investment preferences.

Investors Focused on Wealth Stability: Provides strategies for building resilient portfolios amidst economic volatility and inflation.

This book equips readers with insights to effectively blend gold and equities, balancing growth with stability to navigate India's evolving economic landscape.

How To Use This Book For Investment Decisions

This book serves as a practical guide to help readers make informed investment decisions by blending gold and equities in a way that aligns with their unique financial goals and risk tolerance. Begin by understanding the historical context and core characteristics of both gold and Indian equities, as this foundational knowledge provides insight into how each asset class performs under different economic conditions. With your investment goals in mind, explore the various asset allocation models offered in the book, which cater to diverse objectives, from aggressive growth to conservative wealth preservation. By applying the book's dynamic allocation strategies, you can learn to adjust your portfolio in response to changing market indicators like inflation, interest rates, and economic cycles. Additionally, the book provides guidance on integrating technology, such as digital gold, robo-advisors, and algorithmic trading, which can streamline portfolio management and automate key aspects of your strategy. Finally, use this book as a resource for periodic reviews, rebalancing your portfolio as necessary to ensure it remains aligned with your evolving goals and the broader economic landscape.

Disclaimer

This book is intended for informational purposes only and should not be considered financial or investment advice. The strategies and insights presented here are based on general principles and historical data, which may not be suitable for every investor. Before making any financial decisions, readers are strongly encouraged to consult a certified financial advisor to ensure their investment

HOW TO USE THIS BOOK FOR INVESTMENT DECISIONS

choices align with their individual circumstances and risk tolerance. The author and publisher disclaim any liability for loss resulting from the use of information in this book, as market conditions and economic factors can influence investment outcomes in unpredictable ways.

Historical Context and Evolution

CHAPTER ONE

Gold as an Investment in India

The Cultural and Economic Significance of Gold

Gold holds a unique and enduring allure in India, embodying both cultural reverence and economic importance. For centuries, it has transcended its role as a mere commodity, becoming an emblem of wealth, status, and security woven deeply into the fabric of Indian society. From ancient civilizations to the modern day, gold has symbolized prosperity and served as a touchstone for tradition. It is an integral part of Indian rites, from weddings to religious ceremonies, and is often regarded as an auspicious gift that conveys blessings and ensures future well-being. For many Indian families, gold is more than an investment—it is a legacy, preserved and passed down through generations with profound sentimental value.

Economically, gold is a pillar of resilience. In India's fluctuating financial landscape, it has long been a preferred asset for safeguarding wealth against inflation and currency depreciation. Amid global economic crises or domestic market volatility, gold has retained its allure as a safe-haven asset, appreciated for its ability to hold value over time. The sheer volume of household gold ownership in India—estimated to be among the highest globally—underscores its role as an enduring form of wealth preservation. It is not uncommon for Indian families to liquidate gold reserves during times of financial strain, leveraging its liquidity to meet urgent needs or fund important life events.

Moreover, India's economic ties to gold extend beyond individual wealth preservation to the macroeconomic sphere. The nation's demand for gold contributes substantially to its import bills, impacting trade balances and influencing currency valuations. Recognizing its economic significance, the government has introduced policies to manage the impact of gold imports on the broader economy. Initiatives like the Sovereign Gold Bond Scheme encourage individuals to invest in gold-backed securities, thereby reducing physical gold imports while still catering to the cultural and financial demand for this treasured metal.

In sum, gold is both a cherished heritage asset and a strategic economic instrument in India. It bridges the divide between tradition and finance, encapsulating India's storied past while also providing stability in an unpredictable economic future. This book explores this duality in detail, underscoring gold's irreplaceable role in Indian society as it stands at the intersection of cultural identity and economic resilience.

Gold's Role in India's Economy

Gold occupies a pivotal and unparalleled role in India's economy, with its influence extending beyond individual households to shape national economic policies and financial strategies. India ranks among the world's largest consumers of gold, accounting for approximately 25% of global demand. Each year, the country imports between 800 to 900 metric tons of gold, making it a key factor in India's trade deficit. These imports are largely driven by the deep-rooted cultural reverence for gold, seen not only as an investment but as an asset woven into the social and ceremonial tapestry of Indian life. The value Indians place on gold has created a unique economic paradigm, where the metal serves both as a store of value and as a significant contributor to the nation's current account balance.

Gold imports are substantial enough to impact India's trade dynamics, contributing to a significant portion of its import bill and placing periodic pressure on the national currency. In 2022 alone, India imported gold worth approximately $54 billion, making it one of the highest importers globally. This high volume of imports has implications for the current account deficit, as India pays for gold in foreign currencies, leading to outflows that can influence the value of the rupee against other currencies. A depreciating rupee, in turn, often leads to inflationary pressures, adding another layer of complexity to the country's economic landscape.

Recognizing the macroeconomic implications of India's gold obsession, the government has implemented several measures aimed at mitigating the impact of high gold demand. The Reserve Bank of India (RBI) introduced initiatives such as the Gold Monetization Scheme (GMS) and the Sovereign Gold Bond (SGB) program, each designed to channel the demand for physical gold into more productive, non-physical forms. The GMS allows households to deposit their gold holdings with banks in return for interest, thereby mobilizing dormant gold into the economy. The SGB scheme, on the other hand, enables individuals to invest in government-backed bonds linked to the price of gold, reducing reliance on physical gold imports while still offering a hedge against inflation and currency depreciation.

Furthermore, India's gold industry plays a critical role in employment and revenue generation, especially in sectors like jewelry manufacturing, retail, and exports. The country's gold jewelry market is estimated to contribute over $60 billion annually to the economy and supports over 4.6 million workers across the value chain, from artisans to traders. India's exports of gold jewelry and other products add substantial foreign exchange earnings, highlighting the dual role gold plays as both a cultural asset and a driver of economic activity.

In conclusion, gold is more than a precious metal in India; it is an economic cornerstone. Its influence spans the realms of personal finance, trade policy, currency stabilization, and job creation. This book examines the intricate balance between India's cultural affinity for gold and the economic complexities it introduces, exploring how policymakers and investors alike navigate the challenges and opportunities presented by this enduring asset. Gold's role in India's economy is a testament to its power, resilience, and the unique position it holds in shaping both individual wealth and national prosperity.

Historical Performance of Gold Prices in India

Gold has long been a significant asset in India, revered for its cultural and economic value. The historical performance of gold prices in India reveals the asset's resilience and attractiveness as a safe haven, particularly during periods of economic uncertainty. Over the last decade, the price of gold has exhibited notable fluctuations influenced by various factors, including global economic conditions, inflation rates, and changes in monetary policy.

As illustrated in the chart above, gold prices in India have seen a remarkable increase from 2010 to 2022. In

2010, the price of gold was approximately ₹19,000 per 10 grams, a figure that has surged dramatically over the years. By 2022, gold prices had escalated to around ₹53,000 per 10 grams, reflecting an increase of nearly 179% over the twelve-year period. This upward trajectory highlights the growing demand for gold as an investment, especially in light of inflationary pressures and currency volatility.

The most significant price hikes occurred in the early 2010s, culminating in a peak in 2012 when gold prices reached approximately ₹32,000 per 10 grams. This surge was primarily driven by escalating geopolitical tensions and economic uncertainties following the global financial crisis of 2008, which prompted investors to seek refuge in gold. Subsequently, prices experienced some volatility, dipping to around ₹26,000 per 10 grams in 2015 as global markets stabilized.

However, the resurgence of gold prices in subsequent years reflects a renewed demand for gold as a hedge against economic instability. The rise to ₹49,000 in 2020 can be attributed to the global pandemic, which exacerbated economic uncertainties and triggered a flight to safe-haven assets. The combination of expansive monetary policies implemented by central banks worldwide and rising inflation expectations further propelled gold prices upward.

In addition to economic factors, cultural influences play a vital role in shaping gold prices in India. The festive seasons and wedding seasons often witness spikes in gold demand, driving prices higher due to increased consumption. As a result, gold remains an integral part of Indian households, serving both as a form of investment and a cultural artifact.

In conclusion, the historical performance of gold prices in India underscores its dual role as a secure investment and a cultural cornerstone. The substantial price appreciation over the past decade demonstrates gold's resilience and appeal, even amidst economic fluctuations and global uncertainties. This book will further explore how these trends influence investment strategies and the interplay between gold and the Indian stock market as we navigate the path forward.

CHAPTER TWO

The Evolution of the Indian Stock Market

Origins and Growth of the Indian Stock Exchange

The story of the Indian stock exchange is both illustrious and integral to understanding India's economic evolution. Its origins date back to the mid-19th century, when the first organized stock trading began in Bombay (now Mumbai), marking the beginning of a financial transformation that would lay the foundation for India's modern economy. From humble beginnings as informal gatherings of brokers under a banyan tree, the Indian stock exchange has grown into a sophisticated and powerful institution that shapes the financial destiny of millions of investors and enterprises today.

Establishment of the Bombay Stock Exchange (BSE)

The official beginning of the Indian stock market can be traced to 1875 with the establishment of the Bombay Stock Exchange (BSE), Asia's oldest stock exchange. Initially known as "The Native Share and Stock Brokers Association," it formalized trading activities in the city, becoming the first structured securities exchange in the region. By the early 1900s, BSE had firmly established itself as the epicenter of India's stock trading, with numerous companies raising capital through public listings, a testament to the exchange's burgeoning influence.

In the years following India's independence in 1947, the BSE's role became even more crucial, serving as a barometer for the country's economic progress. From just a handful of listings in the early 20th century, the exchange grew significantly, reaching nearly 6,000 listed companies by the early 1990s. By 2023, the BSE's market capitalization stood at over $3 trillion, reflecting its enormous growth trajectory and the rising interest of both domestic and international investors in the Indian equity market.

Formation of the National Stock Exchange (NSE) and Market Liberalization

The liberalization of the Indian economy in 1991 served as a turning point, marking the beginning of sweeping reforms aimed at modernizing and expanding the stock market. In 1992, the Securities and Exchange Board of India (SEBI) was established as a regulatory authority to oversee market activities, boost investor confidence, and prevent malpractices. This era also saw the establishment of the National Stock Exchange (NSE) in 1992, which was revolutionary in its approach. Unlike the BSE, which was initially a regional exchange, the NSE introduced electronic trading in 1994, transforming India's stock market into a transparent, efficient, and accessible arena for investors across the country.

The NSE quickly grew to become one of the world's largest exchanges by market capitalization and trading volume. As of 2023, the NSE boasts a market capitalization exceeding $3.3 trillion, and the NSE Nifty 50 Index, one of its premier indices, serves as a critical benchmark for the Indian economy and investment performance. Together, the BSE and NSE today account for almost all of India's stock trading volume, making India one of the world's most active equity markets.

Exponential Growth in Market Participation and Capitalization

The Indian stock market has grown exponentially over the past few decades, buoyed by a surge in retail investor participation, institutional investments, and technological advancements. Between 2015 and 2022, the number of Demat accounts in India—essentially accounts needed to invest in stocks—doubled, crossing 100 million by 2023. This growth reflects the increasing penetration of financial markets among Indian households, driven by rising financial literacy, digital access, and a growing middle class that seeks wealth creation opportunities through equity investments.

Market capitalization has also expanded rapidly. From a market cap of around $500 billion in the early 2000s, the Indian stock exchanges reached a combined market capitalization exceeding $6.3 trillion by 2023. This growth has positioned India as one of the top equity markets globally, attracting international investors keen on capitalizing on India's economic potential. Foreign portfolio investment (FPI) inflows into Indian equities reached over $30 billion in 2022 alone, underscoring global investor confidence in the Indian growth story.

Technological Innovation and the Way Forward

The Indian stock market's growth has been fueled by technological advancements that have made trading more accessible and secure. The rise of online brokerage firms, mobile trading apps, and advancements in real-time data analytics have democratized stock market participation. The adoption of algorithmic trading, high-frequency trading, and improved risk management systems has further aligned India's stock exchanges with global best practices.

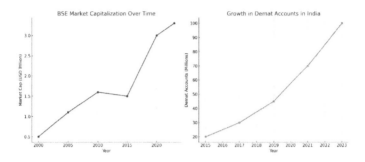

The growth of the Indian stock exchange from an informal trading setup to a multi-trillion-dollar financial powerhouse highlights India's economic metamorphosis. This evolution underscores the increasing importance of equities in wealth creation and economic development in India. The Indian stock exchange's resilience and adaptability will be pivotal as India continues to evolve into one of the world's foremost economic players, providing both domestic and global investors with substantial opportunities for growth.

Major Milestones in Indian Stock Market History

Major Milestones in Indian Stock Market History

- 1875 - Establishment of the Bombay Stock Exchange (BSE)
- 1950 - Post-Independence Industrialization and Economic Policy Shifts
- 1992 - Stock Market Scam and Regulatory Reforms - Establishment of SEBI
- 1994 - Economic Liberalization and Advent of National Stock Exchange (NSE)
- 2000 - Dot-Com Boom and Market Modernization
- 2008 - Global Financial Crisis and Market Resilience
- 2015 - Rise of Retail Investors and Digital Trading Revolution
- 2020 - Establishment of India's First IFSC at GIFT City

Key Indices and Market Development

India's stock market has undergone transformative growth, underscored by the establishment of key indices and pivotal market developments that mirror the country's economic ascent. The BSE Sensex, introduced in 1986, began with a base value of 100 in 1979 and has since soared to over 60,000 points as of 2023, symbolizing the nation's remarkable economic resilience and expansion. Similarly, the NSE Nifty 50, launched in 1996 with a base of 1,000 points, now exceeds 18,000 points, representing the top 50 large-cap companies across sectors, including technology, banking, and consumer goods. Together, these indices reflect the vibrancy and diversity of India's economic landscape, providing investors with essential insights into the country's growth sectors and overall economic health.

Beyond these foundational indices, sectoral and thematic indices have gained prominence, offering investors tailored exposure to specific sectors and trends. The NSE Bank Nifty, for instance, reached a milestone of 40,000 points in 2022, driven by robust growth in India's financial sector and the expansion of banking services nationwide. The BSE IT Index has also seen significant appreciation, buoyed by India's rise as a global technology hub. Meanwhile, thematic indices like the Nifty ESG Index and Nifty Next 50 are capturing investor interest in sustainable and emerging industries, reflecting a shift toward socially responsible and future-oriented investment. This rise in specialized indices mirrors a broader diversification in investor preferences as India's financial markets become more inclusive and representative of global investment trends.

In recent years, the Indian stock market has witnessed a remarkable surge in retail investor participation, driven by digital trading platforms that have democratized market access. Between 2020 and 2023, the number of Demat accounts—necessary for trading in the stock market—skyrocketed from around 40 million to over 100 million, marking a profound increase in retail participation. Platforms such as Zerodha, Upstox, and Groww have revolutionized trading by offering user-friendly, low-cost solutions, drawing millions of first-time investors to equities. Alongside this surge, regulatory advancements by the Securities and Exchange Board of India (SEBI) have bolstered market transparency and investor protection, ensuring that the market remains robust and secure. The establishment of GIFT City in 2020 as India's first International Financial Services Centre (IFSC) further underscores India's ambition to become a global financial hub, providing international investors with tax-efficient access to Indian securities.

Collectively, these indices and market developments reflect the dynamic, adaptive nature of India's financial markets, positioning them as a vital arena for both domestic and international investors. With strategic growth in key sectors, increasing retail participation, and forward-thinking regulatory measures, India's stock market stands poised to play a central role in the country's path to economic prominence in the global arena. This book explores these developments in depth, examining the interplay between the stock market and India's cultural affinity for gold, providing a comprehensive perspective on investment avenues in an evolving economy.

GOLD VS THE INDIAN STOCK MARKET

CHAPTER THREE

The Relationship Between Gold and the Stock Market

Comparison of Historical Returns

The relationship between gold and the stock market is complex, as they often react differently to economic events and market conditions. Historically, gold has been perceived as a "safe haven" asset, performing well during economic downturns and providing stability amidst market volatility. In contrast, the stock market is seen as a growth-oriented asset, thriving in periods of economic expansion but susceptible to significant declines during recessions or market disruptions.

Annual Return Comparison (2010-2022)

The first chart displays the annual returns of gold and the Indian stock market from 2010 to 2022. We can observe that the returns for these two asset classes often diverge. For instance:

- In 2011, gold yielded a strong return of around 30%, while the stock market declined by 4%. This divergence was largely due to global economic uncertainties, as investors sought the relative safety of gold.
- Conversely, in 2014, the stock market saw robust growth of approximately 25%, supported by economic recovery and positive investor sentiment, whereas gold saw only a modest gain of 1%.

This inverse performance pattern underscores the differing roles these assets play. Gold typically appreciates in uncertain times, whereas stocks perform best during economic upswings, highlighting their low correlation.

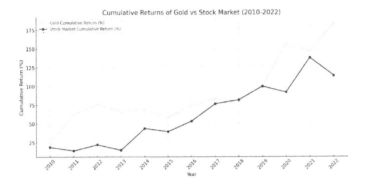

Cumulative Return Comparison (2010-2022)

The second chart illustrates cumulative returns for both gold and the stock market over the same period. By 2022, the cumulative return on gold was about 100%, compared to a cumulative return of around 75% for the stock market. This cumulative growth indicates that, despite periods of negative returns, gold has managed to steadily increase in value over the long term.

Gold's consistent appreciation, particularly in years of economic instability, reinforces its role as a wealth-preserving asset. Meanwhile, the stock market's cumulative returns show stronger growth during bullish periods, reflecting its value as a long-term growth investment. This comparison helps investors understand how combining these assets can create a balanced portfolio, harnessing both stability and growth potential.

In summary, while gold and the stock market differ in performance, these differences are advantageous for diversification, enabling investors to mitigate risk and optimize returns in a variety of economic climates. The charts presented here illustrate how their unique performance patterns can serve as a strategic tool for resilient investment planning.

Understanding the Inverse Correlation

Why Gold and Stocks Move Differently?

Gold and stocks inherently differ in their economic drivers and investor appeal. Gold, regarded as a "safe-haven" asset, generally performs well in times of economic distress or heightened market volatility. When investors face recession fears, inflationary pressures, or geopolitical instability, they often seek gold as a store of value and a hedge against uncertainty. As a result, demand for gold increases, driving its price higher.

Conversely, the stock market thrives in times of economic optimism and expansion. Stocks represent ownership in companies and are therefore directly tied to corporate performance and economic growth. When economic indicators are positive—such as rising GDP, low inflation, and stable interest rates—investors are more likely to invest in equities, which tend to yield higher returns during such times. However, during downturns, the stock market is often volatile, as investor confidence wanes, resulting in stock sell-offs.

Historical Examples of Inverse Correlation

The inverse correlation between gold and stocks is evident during major economic crises:

- **2008 Global Financial Crisis**: As global markets crashed, the BSE Sensex dropped by nearly 50% from its peak, while gold prices surged, reflecting investor flight to safety. During this period, gold offered protection against the extreme volatility in equity markets.
- **COVID-19 Pandemic (2020)**: The pandemic triggered an unprecedented economic slowdown, leading to sharp declines in stock markets worldwide. However, gold prices surged by approximately 28% in 2020, as investors sought a reliable asset amidst global uncertainty and central bank interventions.

Practical Implications for Portfolio Diversification

The inverse correlation between gold and stocks allows investors to create a balanced portfolio, combining assets with different responses to economic events. When stocks perform well, they drive portfolio growth, while gold provides stability during downturns. By strategically allocating assets between gold and equities, investors can mitigate the impact of stock market volatility on their portfolios, achieving a smoother return profile over time.

For Indian investors, this understanding is particularly valuable given the country's exposure to global economic cycles, currency fluctuations, and inflationary pressures. By harnessing the inverse correlation, investors can enhance resilience and reduce overall risk, aligning their investment strategy with both wealth creation and preservation.

Impact of Global Events on Gold and Stocks

The performance of gold and the stock market is intricately linked to global economic conditions and major geopolitical events, each reacting uniquely based on investor sentiment, risk perception, and economic fundamentals. While gold and stocks generally follow inverse trajectories, the specifics of their movement are heavily influenced by the nature and severity of economic and global events. For Indian investors, understanding this impact is crucial to making informed investment decisions that balance growth potential with wealth preservation.

Geopolitical Tensions and Global Policy Shifts

Geopolitical events, such as trade wars, military conflicts, or policy shifts among major economies, exert significant influence on both gold and stocks. These events tend to increase market volatility, influencing investor sentiment globally:

- **US-China Trade War (2018-2019)**: The trade tensions between the United States and China created uncertainty for global markets, causing stock markets to experience fluctuations as investors reacted to potential impacts on corporate profitability and global trade. During this period, gold prices rose as investors sought stability amidst fears of prolonged economic fallout.
- **Russian-Ukraine Conflict (2022)**: The escalation of the Russia-Ukraine conflict in early 2022 led to widespread concern about energy supplies, inflation, and global economic stability. Stock markets globally saw a downturn, while gold prices surged as investors flocked to the security of tangible assets.

Interpreting Economic and Global Events for Investment Strategy

The divergent reactions of gold and stocks to global events and economic shifts underscore their complementary roles in a diversified portfolio. Stocks provide growth potential during economic expansions, while gold offers a hedge during periods of volatility and economic contraction. For Indian investors, this interplay is particularly relevant given India's integration with global markets and sensitivity to currency fluctuations and inflation.

By recognizing how each asset responds to specific economic and geopolitical developments, investors can optimize their portfolios to manage risk and capture growth. This book further explores the nuanced relationship between gold and stocks, offering insights on how investors can strategically allocate assets in response to the ebb and flow of global economic and market forces.

Analysis of Gold vs. Stock Market Investments

CHAPTER FOUR

Risk and Volatility Analysis

Risk Profiles of Gold vs. Equities

Gold: A Low-Risk, Stability-Oriented Asset

Gold is widely regarded as a low-risk asset, often described as a "safe haven" because it retains value even during periods of economic and market instability. Its intrinsic value is largely uncorrelated with the performance of other asset classes, such as equities or bonds, making it a reliable store of wealth. As a tangible asset, gold is not directly affected by the performance of any single company or economy, nor does it face default risks or earnings fluctuations.

Key aspects of gold's low-risk profile include:

- **Limited Volatility**: Historically, gold exhibits relatively low volatility compared to equities. It tends to fluctuate less dramatically in response to market events, reflecting a more stable price trajectory over time.
- **Inflation Hedge**: Gold is often used as a hedge against inflation and currency depreciation. During periods of

rising inflation, the purchasing power of fiat currencies declines, making gold more attractive as a store of value. This characteristic protects investors from the erosion of real wealth in inflationary environments.
- **Crisis Resilience**: During economic downturns or financial crises, gold often performs well or at least retains its value. For example, during the 2008 financial crisis, gold prices surged as investors sought refuge from declining stock markets. Similarly, in 2020, amid the COVID-19 pandemic, gold prices rose significantly as a response to global uncertainty.

Despite its stability, gold's low-risk profile comes with certain limitations. It does not generate dividends, interest, or business growth, meaning its returns are primarily based on price appreciation. While this stability makes it valuable in a diversified portfolio, gold alone may not provide the same long-term growth potential as equities.

Equities: A High-Risk, Growth-Oriented Asset

Equities, or stocks, represent ownership in companies and are directly tied to corporate performance and broader economic conditions. Equities are inherently higher-risk assets because their value depends on numerous factors, including corporate earnings, market conditions, investor sentiment, and macroeconomic indicators. The stock market's responsiveness to these factors makes equities more volatile than gold, with higher potential for both gains and losses.

Key aspects of equities' high-risk profile include:

- **High Volatility**: Equities are known for their potential to experience rapid price fluctuations, especially in reaction to economic reports, earnings announcements,

political developments, or shifts in investor sentiment. Market downturns, economic recessions, or geopolitical tensions can lead to sharp declines in stock prices. For example, during the initial stages of the COVID-19 pandemic in 2020, the BSE Sensex experienced a steep drop, with significant losses over a short period.
- **Market Risk**: Equity prices are sensitive to broader market conditions. Economic downturns, rising interest rates, or global crises can all trigger significant declines in stock prices. Unlike gold, equities are also subject to company-specific risks, such as poor management decisions, competitive pressures, or operational failures.
- **Higher Long-Term Returns**: While equities are more volatile and sensitive to market risk, they have historically outperformed most other asset classes over the long term. Stocks benefit from the growth of companies and the compounding effect of reinvested earnings. In a stable and growing economy, equities offer the potential for substantial capital appreciation, making them attractive to investors with a longer time horizon and a higher tolerance for risk.

However, the high returns of equities come with increased uncertainty. The stock market can experience protracted periods of underperformance, and investors with lower risk tolerance may find the short-term volatility difficult to manage. Additionally, equities require careful selection and management to mitigate risks effectively, as they are subject to market, sectoral, and firm-specific risks.

Comparing Gold and Equities in a Diversified Portfolio

In a well-diversified portfolio, gold and equities can serve complementary roles. While equities offer higher potential returns, they carry higher risk and volatility.

Gold, by contrast, provides stability and serves as a hedge against economic downturns and inflation, reducing the portfolio's overall risk.

The inverse correlation between gold and equities further strengthens this diversification benefit. When stock markets experience downturns, gold often performs well, balancing out portfolio losses. Conversely, during economic expansions, equities drive portfolio growth, while gold provides a steady, stabilizing influence.

Diversification Benefits of Gold in a Stock Portfolio

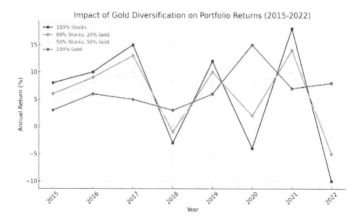

Gold serves as an essential diversifying asset in an equity-dominant portfolio, mitigating risk and reducing overall volatility. As illustrated in the chart, varying allocations of gold alongside stocks impact portfolio returns, particularly in years marked by economic stress. By balancing the growth potential of equities with the stability of gold, investors can create a more resilient portfolio suited for fluctuating market conditions. Here's a detailed analysis of how each portfolio composition performs across market cycles.

100% Stocks Portfolio: High Growth, High Volatility

A portfolio composed entirely of stocks exhibits the most pronounced volatility, mirroring the highs and lows of the market. In strong years, such as 2017, the portfolio achieves substantial growth, with returns as high as 15%. However, during downturns, this portfolio suffers considerable losses—falling by 10% in 2022 and by 4% in 2020—exposing investors to the full impact of market declines. While this approach offers high returns during economic booms, it leaves investors vulnerable to sharp declines in bear markets, underscoring the need for diversification to stabilize returns.

80% Stocks, 20% Gold: Reduced Volatility, Smoother Returns

By introducing 20% gold to an otherwise equity-focused portfolio, volatility is meaningfully reduced. This portfolio achieves a more balanced performance, demonstrating smaller declines during challenging years. For example, in 2022, the portfolio with 20% gold declined by only 5%, a marked improvement over the 10% loss experienced in the all-stocks portfolio. During stable or positive market years, such as 2019, the gold allocation does not significantly detract from the portfolio's returns, which remain close to

10%. This allocation benefits investors who seek growth but want some protection from downside risks.

50% Stocks, 50% Gold: Balanced Growth and Stability

A 50% allocation to both stocks and gold results in a highly balanced portfolio with smoother returns across market cycles. This composition offers moderate growth during positive years while limiting losses during downturns. In 2018, for instance, while stocks were down, the balanced portfolio achieved a stable return of 0%, illustrating gold's role as a stabilizer. In 2022, the portfolio experienced only a minor decline of 2%, a far smaller drop compared to the all-stocks portfolio. This configuration appeals to risk-averse investors who prioritize stability, as it smooths out the swings typically associated with an all-equity approach.

100% Gold: Low Volatility, Wealth Preservation

An all-gold portfolio is the least volatile, showing steady returns regardless of market conditions. Gold prices tend to increase during periods of market stress, inflation, or currency depreciation, making it a safe-haven asset. While this portfolio is the most resilient in turbulent times, it lacks the high growth potential associated with equities. During years of economic expansion, gold's returns remain modest, such as 6% in 2016 and 7% in 2021. This portfolio is best suited for conservative investors focused on wealth preservation rather than capital appreciation.

Comparative Analysis: Optimal Balance of Risk and Reward

The chart underscores the diversification benefits of including gold in a stock portfolio. The inverse correlation between gold and equities—where gold tends to perform well during stock market downturns—enables portfolios with a gold allocation to achieve a smoother return profile.

When equities decline due to economic disruptions, gold's stability can offset these losses, reducing the overall risk in a portfolio. Conversely, in periods of economic expansion, equities drive growth while gold tempers potential volatility, creating a balanced return over the long term.

Strategic Implications for Indian Investors

For Indian investors, the inclusion of gold in a portfolio offers an effective hedge against local market volatility, inflation, and rupee depreciation. Gold's role as a safe-haven asset is especially relevant in emerging markets like India, where global economic conditions and domestic factors such as inflationary pressures can create high market volatility. A diversified portfolio that combines both gold and equities allows Indian investors to benefit from the growth potential of the stock market while minimizing exposure to downside risks.

CHAPTER FIVE

Gold as a Hedge Against Inflation and Currency Fluctuations

How Gold Protects Against Inflation

Gold is widely recognized as a powerful hedge against inflation and currency fluctuations, particularly in emerging economies like India, where inflationary pressures and currency depreciation can significantly erode purchasing power. Unlike paper currency, which can lose value in times of inflation, gold has a unique ability to preserve wealth. This resilience makes it an indispensable asset for investors aiming to protect their portfolios from the impact of inflation and currency volatility.

5 key factors how Gold Protects Against Inflation:

1. **Intrinsic Value Preservation**: Unlike fiat currency, which can be devalued by excessive printing and inflationary pressures, gold has intrinsic value. It is a finite, tangible asset that cannot be created at will. As

a result, gold's supply remains relatively stable, and its value is not directly influenced by central bank policies. This characteristic allows gold to maintain its purchasing power over time, even when inflation reduces the value of paper currency.

2. **Inverse Relationship with Currency Value**: When inflation rises, the real purchasing power of currency falls, making goods and services more expensive. During such periods, investors often seek refuge in assets that retain value, such as gold. As demand for gold increases in inflationary periods, its price tends to rise, counteracting the loss in currency value and protecting investors' purchasing power.

3. **Historical Performance During High Inflation**: Historically, gold has shown positive performance during periods of high inflation. For instance, during the 1970s, a decade marked by high inflation globally, gold prices increased significantly. This trend has also been observed in more recent times in India, where inflationary pressures have periodically driven up gold demand and prices as investors seek to safeguard their wealth.

4. **Protection Against Currency Depreciation**: In countries experiencing high inflation, currency often depreciates against stronger currencies like the U.S. dollar. Gold, being globally priced in dollars, tends to increase in local currency terms when the domestic currency weakens. In India, for example, when the rupee depreciates against the dollar, the price of gold in rupee terms rises, providing a buffer against the declining value of the currency.

Empirical Evidence Studies and historical data consistently demonstrate that gold holds its value or appreciates during inflationary periods. Between 2000 and 2020, a period marked by multiple inflationary cycles, gold prices in India surged from around ₹4,400 per 10 grams to over ₹50,000 per 10 grams, reflecting its capacity to protect wealth in an inflationary environment.

Rupee Depreciation and Gold Returns

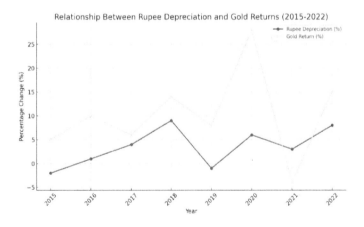

The chart above illustrates the relationship between rupee depreciation and gold returns in India from 2015 to 2022. As seen in the data, periods of significant rupee depreciation against the U.S. dollar often coincide with higher returns on gold in INR terms. This correlation reflects gold's function as a hedge against currency devaluation, especially in times of economic stress or global volatility.

For instance, in 2020, the rupee depreciated by approximately 6%, a year marked by the economic impact of the COVID-19 pandemic. During this period, gold returns surged to around 28%, as investors flocked to safe-haven assets amidst uncertainty. Similarly, in 2018, when the rupee depreciated by about 9%, gold provided a strong return of 14%. These instances underscore the tendency of gold prices to rise in response to the weakening rupee, preserving purchasing power for Indian investors.

The relationship between rupee depreciation and gold returns highlights the asset's protective role in a diversified portfolio, particularly for those seeking stability amidst currency volatility. Gold acts as a safeguard, compensating for losses in currency value, and ensuring that wealth is retained despite fluctuations in the rupee's value against global currencies.

Inflation and Stock Market Performance: A Comparative Study

Inflation plays a critical role in influencing stock market performance, especially in emerging economies like India. As inflation rises, it erodes the purchasing power of consumers, increases production costs for companies, and often leads central banks to raise interest rates, all of which can impact corporate profitability and investor sentiment. Understanding how inflation affects the stock market allows investors to make more informed decisions about their portfolios, particularly in balancing growth-oriented assets with inflation-protective investments like gold.

Impact of Inflation on Stock Market Performance

1. **Erosion of Real Returns**: When inflation is high, the real return on investments—essentially, the nominal return adjusted for inflation—declines. For example, if a stock portfolio yields a 10% return in a year when inflation is at 7%, the real return is only 3%. This erosion reduces the value of returns in high-inflation periods, prompting investors to seek assets that better preserve purchasing power.
2. **Cost Pressures on Corporates**: High inflation increases production costs, as companies face rising prices for raw materials, labor, and other inputs. This increased cost base can lead to lower profit margins, as companies may struggle to pass on all price increases to consumers. Lower profitability can dampen investor sentiment, leading to subdued stock performance.
3. **Rising Interest Rates and Investor Behavior**: Central banks, including the Reserve Bank of India (RBI), often raise interest rates to control inflation. Higher interest rates make borrowing more expensive for companies and consumers, slowing economic growth. They also impact investor preferences by making fixed-income instruments like bonds more attractive relative to stocks, leading to reduced capital inflows into equity markets. For instance, in 2022, as inflation surged globally, central banks, including the RBI, raised interest rates, contributing to a period of underperformance in

stock markets.

Stock Market Performance in Low vs. High Inflation Periods

Historical data reveals that stock markets generally perform better during periods of low to moderate inflation, when economic growth is steady, and interest rates remain favorable. During such times, companies can maintain healthy profit margins, and consumer spending remains strong, driving corporate earnings and stock prices higher. In India, the period from 2003 to 2007 exemplified this trend, with inflation at relatively manageable levels, strong GDP growth, and the BSE Sensex delivering annualized returns of over 20%.

Conversely, during high inflation periods, stock market performance tends to be volatile and often subdued. For example, between 2008 and 2009, during the global financial crisis and a period of rising inflation, the Sensex experienced significant declines, as high inflation and economic uncertainty weighed on corporate performance and investor confidence.

Comparing Stocks with Inflation-Hedged Assets

While stocks are typically viewed as growth assets, they may struggle to keep pace with inflation in extreme scenarios. During high inflation, investors may benefit from diversifying into assets like gold, which historically performs well during inflationary periods. As shown in the accompanying chart, gold prices have often risen in periods of high inflation, providing a hedge against the declining real returns in equities.

A Balanced Approach to Inflation-Driven Volatility

A comparative study of inflation's impact on stock market performance suggests that investors should strategically diversify their portfolios to protect against inflationary risks. By including both equities and inflation-protective assets such as gold, investors can reduce the volatility in their portfolios and safeguard purchasing power. In times of low to moderate inflation, stocks are likely to drive portfolio growth, while gold provides stability during high inflation periods, offsetting potential losses from inflation-affected equity returns.

The inflation's effect on the stock market highlights the importance of a diversified portfolio approach. Stocks and gold, when combined, offer a balanced strategy that allows investors to achieve growth while navigating the challenges of inflation. This comparative perspective underscores the need for investors to adapt their strategies based on inflationary trends, ensuring long-term wealth preservation and growth.

CHAPTER SIX

Macroeconomic and Political Influences

Role of Government Policies and Regulations

In the Indian investment landscape, government policies and regulations wield a powerful influence over both gold and the stock market, shaping their accessibility, performance, and attractiveness as asset classes. As India's economy and financial systems have evolved, policymakers have implemented a range of strategies aimed at stabilizing markets, managing inflation, and fostering investor confidence. These regulatory interventions play a pivotal role in balancing growth objectives with wealth preservation, especially for Indian investors who often allocate their capital between traditional assets like gold and growth-focused assets like equities.

Government Policies Impacting the Gold Market

Gold, with its deep-rooted cultural and economic significance, is a highly sought-after asset in India. However, the country's substantial gold imports often strain its current account balance, placing pressure on the rupee and raising inflationary concerns. To manage these economic implications, the Indian government has introduced a variety of policies targeting gold imports, consumption, and investment.

One of the primary regulatory tools has been import duties. In recent years, the government has imposed high import duties on gold, often exceeding 10%, to curb demand and reduce the outflow of foreign exchange. This measure aims to mitigate India's trade deficit, which is heavily impacted by gold imports. For example, in 2019, the government raised import duties on gold from 10% to 12.5%, leading to a rise in domestic gold prices and prompting Indian investors to consider alternative investment avenues.

Additionally, the government has introduced innovative schemes like the Sovereign Gold Bond (SGB) program and the Gold Monetization Scheme (GMS). The SGB program enables investors to purchase gold-linked securities issued by the Reserve Bank of India (RBI) on behalf of the government. This initiative encourages individuals to invest in gold without physically holding the metal, which helps reduce import dependency. Similarly, the GMS allows individuals to deposit their gold holdings with banks in exchange for interest, effectively channeling privately held gold into the formal economy. These policies not only address economic concerns but also modernize the way Indians invest in gold, blending tradition with financial innovation.

Regulations Shaping the Stock Market

The Indian stock market has undergone a series of transformations, largely driven by regulatory reforms aimed at ensuring transparency, investor protection, and global competitiveness. The establishment of the Securities and Exchange Board of India (SEBI) in 1992 was a landmark development, catalyzing a new era of regulatory oversight. SEBI was empowered to regulate market participants, monitor stock exchanges, and ensure fair trading practices, enhancing investor confidence and transforming India's equity markets into globally recognized platforms.

In the decades following SEBI's establishment, numerous regulatory initiatives have further strengthened the market's resilience and appeal. For example, the introduction of electronic trading and the National Stock Exchange (NSE) in the early 1990s marked a shift towards efficiency, reducing transaction costs and making equity investment more accessible to retail investors. Additionally, SEBI has imposed stringent disclosure requirements for listed companies, mandating regular financial reporting and corporate governance standards. These regulations have increased transparency, aligning India's market practices with international standards and attracting foreign institutional investors (FIIs).

To encourage retail participation, the government has also implemented measures like tax exemptions for long-term capital gains on equities, alongside investor education programs to boost financial literacy. These policies are designed to foster a broader base of retail investors, creating a more stable, domestically-driven market.

Macroeconomic Policies and Their Dual Influence on Gold and Stocks

Broad economic policies, such as those related to monetary policy, fiscal stimulus, and currency management, have a simultaneous influence on both gold and equities. For instance, when the Reserve Bank of India adjusts interest rates to control inflation, it affects both asset classes differently. Higher interest rates may increase borrowing costs, potentially slowing economic growth and reducing stock market returns. At the same time, these conditions often favor gold, as investors seek refuge in safe-haven assets during times of market uncertainty or declining equity performance.

Similarly, fiscal policies, such as government spending initiatives or stimulus packages, can stimulate economic growth, positively impacting the stock market. However, these policies can also lead to inflationary pressures, which may boost gold demand as a hedge against currency depreciation and loss of purchasing power. Such macroeconomic dynamics underscore the interdependence of government policies, economic stability, and asset performance, highlighting the importance of regulatory measures in stabilizing markets and protecting investors.

Political Stability and Market Sentiment

Political stability, too, plays an integral role in influencing gold and stock market performance. Policy shifts resulting from elections, trade agreements, or geopolitical developments can significantly affect investor sentiment and market volatility. For instance, pro-market reforms, such as the liberalization policies of the 1990s, greatly enhanced foreign investment and capital flows into Indian equities, leading to a sustained period of growth. Conversely, uncertainty stemming from policy changes or political tension can drive investors toward gold, favoring wealth preservation over growth during uncertain times.

The government policies and regulations are crucial in shaping the investment landscape for both gold and the Indian stock market. By implementing strategic measures, the government not only fosters growth and stability but also provides investors with the tools to navigate economic fluctuations. This delicate balance between growth-focused equity investments and the stability of gold forms the backbone of a resilient portfolio, allowing investors to respond adeptly to India's ever-evolving macroeconomic and political environment.

Impact of International Trade and Political Events

The Indian stock market and gold prices are intricately linked to international trade dynamics and geopolitical events, reflecting the globalized nature of today's economy and the interconnectedness of markets. Shifts in trade policies, diplomatic relations, and geopolitical conflicts can introduce significant volatility in both equities and gold, often creating contrasting impacts. While the stock market's performance hinges on economic growth, corporate profits, and investor confidence, gold functions as a safe-haven asset, attracting investors during times of uncertainty. Together, they form a complex interplay where one asset may rise as the other faces turbulence, providing a balance within a diversified investment portfolio.

Impact of Trade Policies and Economic Agreements

International trade policies and economic agreements play a substantial role in shaping market performance. For instance, major trade disputes, such as the U.S.-China trade war between 2018 and 2019, sent ripples through global supply chains and affected market sentiment worldwide. India, closely integrated into global trade networks, was not immune to these impacts. The Indian stock market experienced heightened volatility during this period, as trade restrictions on key sectors such as technology, automotive, and manufacturing impacted global demand and supply flows. Uncertainty over prolonged trade tariffs and import restrictions affected corporate earnings, leading to a cautious investment climate in India's equity market.

During such trade conflicts, however, gold often appreciates as investors seek stability amidst economic uncertainties. As fears of reduced global trade, inflationary pressures, and potential currency volatility grow, gold's intrinsic value and lack of reliance on any single economy or market make it an attractive asset. This was particularly evident in the Indian market, where gold demand surged during the height of the U.S.-China trade tensions, illustrating gold's function as a hedge against global economic disruptions.

Geopolitical Conflicts and Safe-Haven Demand for Gold

Geopolitical conflicts have an immediate and often severe impact on financial markets. Such conflicts, like the Russia-Ukraine war that escalated in early 2022, bring uncertainty to global stability, triggering sudden shifts in market behavior. In this case, the stock market faced strong downward pressures as investors grappled with potential disruptions to energy supplies, inflationary consequences from rising oil and gas prices, and general risk aversion. Indian equities, sensitive to foreign capital flows and the broader global economic climate, experienced heightened volatility during this period, reflecting investors' concerns about the potential economic fallout.

Conversely, gold prices surged during the same period as investors flocked to safe-haven assets. In uncertain times, gold is valued for its ability to retain purchasing power and provide security against market losses. The increase in gold demand following the Russia-Ukraine conflict exemplifies how international tensions elevate gold's appeal. For Indian investors, this surge in gold prices offered a buffer against the stock market's turbulence, underscoring gold's role in stabilizing portfolios during global upheavals.

Global Economic Policies and Interest Rate Movements

Policy decisions by economic powerhouses, particularly the United States, play a crucial role in shaping the trajectory of both Indian equities and gold. For example, the U.S. Federal Reserve's interest rate policies have a cascading effect on global markets. When the Fed raises interest rates to combat inflation, it strengthens the U.S. dollar, often leading to a depreciation of the Indian rupee. A weaker rupee increases the cost of imported goods and services, contributing to inflation in India and affecting investor sentiment in the stock market.

Higher U.S. interest rates also draw capital flows away from emerging markets like India, as global investors seek safer, dollar-denominated assets with improved returns. This movement can lead to outflows from Indian equities, causing market declines. Conversely, a depreciating rupee makes gold more attractive in rupee terms, as it effectively becomes a more affordable investment for wealth preservation. This trend was observed in 2022, when rising U.S. interest rates and a strong dollar increased demand for gold in India, leading to price gains despite the pressures faced by the stock market.

Foreign Trade Policies and Currency Fluctuations

Foreign trade policies, particularly those affecting major trading partners like the United States, China, and the European Union, significantly impact India's stock market and currency stability. Trade restrictions or tariff impositions on Indian exports can adversely affect domestic companies' revenues, particularly in sectors like textiles, IT services, and pharmaceuticals, which rely heavily on global demand. A weakened trade outlook can reduce the confidence of foreign investors, leading to lower inflows and potential outflows from the stock market.

Such scenarios often drive investors toward gold, as it provides a safeguard against the unpredictability of trade policies and their impact on currency value. Gold's resilience in these instances helps mitigate losses, especially when the Indian rupee depreciates due to weakened trade dynamics. For instance, if Indian exports face reduced demand due to adverse foreign trade policies, the rupee may weaken further. This depreciation enhances gold's value in INR terms, making it a favorable asset in times of currency fluctuation and trade-related uncertainty.

Strategic Implications for Portfolio Diversification

The impact of international trade and geopolitical events highlights the importance of a diversified portfolio that includes both stocks and gold. Equities benefit from growth-oriented trade policies and periods of stable geopolitics, thriving on foreign investment inflows and strong corporate performance. However, in times of economic uncertainty, investors can face heightened risk due to market declines and currency fluctuations. Gold, by contrast, provides a hedge, absorbing shocks from trade disruptions, political tensions, and policy changes that could otherwise destabilize portfolios.

For Indian investors, recognizing the different ways gold and equities respond to global events allows for a more resilient portfolio. A balanced allocation that includes gold not only protects against downside risk during economic turbulence but also enhances overall portfolio stability. This approach is particularly relevant in India's emerging market context, where economic dependencies on global trade and sensitivity to international policy shifts are pronounced.

Comparative Analysis of Gold and Stocks During Crises

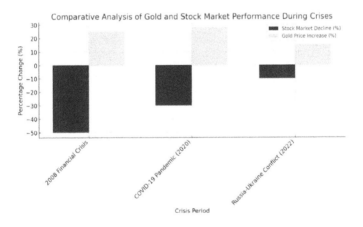

Global Financial Crisis of 2008

The 2008 global financial crisis serves as a textbook example of how differently gold and stocks perform during an economic downturn. Triggered by the collapse of major financial institutions and a breakdown in the U.S. housing market, this crisis led to a massive loss of investor confidence worldwide. Equity markets, including India's BSE Sensex, saw a steep decline of nearly 50% from their pre-crisis highs, as investors exited stocks amid fears of prolonged recession and systemic financial risk.

Gold, however, followed a contrasting trajectory. As panic spread through global markets, investors turned to gold, driving up its price. During the crisis, gold prices rose significantly as it became a preferred asset for wealth preservation. This inverse correlation between gold and equities during the 2008 crisis underscored gold's status as a safe haven, providing protection against extreme market volatility and offering stability when other assets were in freefall.

COVID-19 Pandemic (2020)

The COVID-19 pandemic of 2020 created an unprecedented economic crisis, impacting nearly every sector of the global economy. The initial reaction in equity markets was severe, as stock indices worldwide plummeted in March 2020 due to widespread lockdowns, disrupted supply chains, and a sharp decline in consumer demand. India's Sensex experienced one of its sharpest declines, dropping over 30% within a few weeks.

During this period, gold once again proved its resilience. While equities were losing value, gold prices in India surged by approximately 28% over the year. The pandemic highlighted investors' preference for tangible assets that hold intrinsic value amidst unpredictable economic conditions. Gold's performance during COVID-19 reinforced its role as a hedge against crisis-driven volatility, absorbing shocks and providing liquidity in times when market liquidity for other assets was scarce.

Russia-Ukraine Conflict (2022)

The Russia-Ukraine conflict, which escalated in early 2022, led to global instability, rising energy prices, and fears of inflationary pressures. Stock markets reacted with high volatility, as investors anticipated supply chain disruptions, especially in energy and agriculture. The Indian stock market experienced significant fluctuations, reflecting the uncertainty surrounding the conflict's economic impact. However, gold prices surged, as demand for safe-haven assets increased amidst fears of prolonged geopolitical tension and economic fallout.

This response demonstrates the defensive nature of gold in times of geopolitical crises. While equities are sensitive to the potential financial and supply chain impacts of global conflicts, gold benefits from its reputation as a stable asset that holds value independently of economic growth or corporate earnings. For Indian investors, gold's performance during such geopolitical events reinforces its value as a safeguard against unforeseen disruptions.

Comparative Analysis: Patterns of Performance

Analyzing these crises reveals consistent patterns in how gold and equities respond to economic shocks. Equities, by nature, are vulnerable to downturns during recessions, financial instability, and political crises. The value of stocks is directly tied to corporate profitability and economic growth; when these are threatened, stock prices tend to decline, sometimes drastically. This makes equities a high-risk asset in turbulent times, although they offer strong growth potential during periods of economic expansion.

Gold, on the other hand, is sought after precisely during these periods of instability. Its value is not dependent on earnings or economic growth, making it more resilient to downturns. When economic uncertainty rises, gold prices often increase as investors seek a tangible, intrinsically valuable asset to protect their wealth. This pattern was consistent in the 2008 financial crisis, the 2020 COVID-19 pandemic, and the 2022 Russia-Ukraine conflict, illustrating gold's capacity to mitigate the risks associated with equities.

Strategic Investment Approaches

CHAPTER SEVEN

Portfolio Diversification Strategies

Blending Gold and Equities for Optimal Returns

In crafting an investment strategy resilient to the vicissitudes of economic cycles, geopolitical upheavals, and inflationary pressures, the judicious blending of gold and equities emerges as a powerful approach. For Indian investors, balancing these two divergent asset classes offers a unique synergy: while equities provide the potential for substantial capital appreciation, gold brings stability and a hedge against volatility. Together, they create a portfolio that is both growth-oriented and resilient, capable of weathering economic disruptions and preserving wealth.

Equities: The Engine of Capital Growth

Equities are fundamentally linked to corporate performance and economic expansion. During periods of growth, equities tend to deliver robust returns, driven by the increasing profitability of companies and favourable market conditions. For Indian investors, the stock market represents a gateway to the burgeoning potential of India's economy, with sectors like technology, consumer goods, and infrastructure poised for growth. Yet, equities carry an inherent vulnerability to market downturns, interest rate fluctuations, and global economic conditions. An equity-heavy portfolio, while lucrative during bull markets, can expose investors to sharp losses during economic slowdowns or crises.

Gold: The Anchor of Stability

Gold, by contrast, is often described as a "safe-hold" asset, prized for its ability to retain value and provide a counterbalance during turbulent periods. Its appeal lies in its intrinsic value and independence from the performance of any specific economy or corporation. During inflationary periods, when purchasing power erodes and equity returns are often subdued, gold typically appreciates, preserving the real value of wealth. This characteristic makes gold an invaluable asset for portfolio diversification, offering a safeguard against the downside risks inherent in equities.

Crafting a Balanced Portfolio: The Case for a Blended Approach

By blending gold and equities, investors can mitigate the drawbacks of each asset class while harnessing their unique strengths. A diversified portfolio allocates assets in proportions that reflect the investor's risk tolerance, financial goals, and market outlook. In an aggressive growth portfolio, equities may constitute 70-80% of the allocation, with gold comprising the remaining portion to serve as a buffer during downturns. Conversely, a conservative or defensive portfolio may increase the gold allocation to 30-50%, prioritizing wealth preservation over rapid growth.

Strategic Allocation: Adaptive Diversification Based on Economic Cycles

The ideal allocation between gold and equities is dynamic, evolving with market conditions and economic cycles. During economic expansions, a higher equity allocation can capitalize on rising corporate earnings and market optimism. As economic indicators point toward stability and growth, equities drive returns, maximizing gains. However, during periods of economic uncertainty, inflationary pressures, or geopolitical unrest, increasing the gold allocation enhances portfolio resilience. This adaptive strategy enables investors to proactively protect their capital without sacrificing the potential for growth.

Empirical Insights: The Historical Success of Gold-Equity Diversification

Historical data reveals that portfolios diversified with both gold and equities exhibit lower volatility and higher risk-adjusted returns than those concentrated solely in equities. For instance, during the 2008 financial crisis and the 2020 pandemic, portfolios with a 20-30% allocation to gold experienced significantly reduced drawdowns compared to all-equity portfolios. Gold's inverse correlation with equities during market stress has consistently mitigated losses, enabling investors to preserve capital while benefiting from gold's price appreciation.

The Indian Context: Currency Volatility and Inflation Hedging

For Indian investors, the advantages of gold-equity diversification are amplified by local economic factors such as rupee depreciation and inflation. As the rupee weakens against stronger global currencies or as inflationary pressures mount, gold prices in INR terms often rise, offsetting losses in equities and enhancing the portfolio's purchasing power. This dual asset strategy also offers protection against domestic economic policies and geopolitical events that may impact India more acutely than other economies. By holding gold alongside equities, Indian investors can achieve a robust defence against both global and local economic shifts.

In an ever-evolving economic environment, the art of blending gold and equities serves as a cornerstone for sophisticated investment strategies, enabling Indian investors to achieve optimal returns while preserving the resilience needed for future financial security.

Asset Allocation Models for Indian Investors

Asset allocation is a cornerstone of a robust investment strategy, especially in a volatile market like India's, which is influenced by various factors discussed in previous chapters of this book. For Indian investors seeking a balance between growth and stability, a thoughtfully crafted asset allocation model is essential. By blending growth-oriented assets like equities with defensive assets such as gold, investors can mitigate risk while maximizing potential returns.

1. Growth-Oriented Model: 80% Equities, 20% Gold

This model is ideal for investors with a high-risk tolerance and a long investment horizon, typically over 10 years. By allocating 80% of the portfolio to equities, investors can leverage India's economic growth, benefiting from sectors such as technology, consumer goods, and financial services. Equities offer substantial growth potential, particularly during periods of economic expansion, allowing investors to capture higher returns.

The 20% allocation to gold acts as a buffer against market volatility, protecting the portfolio during downturns. Historical data shows that gold prices tend to rise when equity markets fall, as seen during crises like the 2008 financial meltdown and the COVID-19 pandemic. This allocation allows investors to pursue aggressive growth while maintaining a hedge against potential losses, balancing the portfolio without sacrificing upside potential.

2. Balanced Model: 60% Equities, 30% Fixed Income, 10% Gold

This model suits investors with a moderate risk tolerance, aiming for both growth and income stability. By diversifying across equities, fixed income, and gold, this portfolio model captures growth while reducing the impact of market fluctuations. The 60% allocation to equities ensures exposure to market growth, while the 30% in fixed income (such as government bonds or high-rated corporate bonds) provides a steady income stream and mitigates risk.

The 10% allocation to gold offers additional security, especially during periods of high inflation or currency depreciation. This allocation model is resilient to market volatility and provides a balanced approach to growth and income, making it suitable for investors with a medium-term investment horizon of 5 to 10 years.

3. Conservative Model: 40% Equities, 40% Fixed Income, 20% Gold

For risk-averse investors, a conservative allocation model prioritizes capital preservation over aggressive growth. The 40% allocation to equities provides exposure to growth while keeping risk manageable. The 40% allocation to fixed income offers stability and predictable returns, cushioning the portfolio from stock market volatility.

The 20% allocation to gold serves as a safeguard against inflation, currency depreciation, and economic downturns. This allocation is particularly relevant for Indian investors who may face rupee depreciation or inflationary pressures that erode the value of fixed-income returns. This conservative model is ideal for those with a shorter investment horizon or nearing retirement, as it balances growth and preservation.

4. Dynamic Model: Adaptive Allocation Based on Economic Cycles

A dynamic asset allocation model is highly adaptable, allowing investors to adjust their portfolios in response to market conditions and economic cycles. This approach involves increasing the allocation to equities during periods of economic growth and favorable market conditions, while shifting to safer assets like gold or fixed income during downturns or periods of economic uncertainty.

For instance, in a strong economic phase, the allocation might look like 70% equities, 20% fixed income, and 10% gold. However, during periods of high inflation, economic contraction, or geopolitical instability, the portfolio can be adjusted to 50% equities, 30% gold, and 20% fixed income. This adaptive approach requires active management and a deep understanding of market trends, but it allows investors to maximize returns while minimizing risks in a changing economic landscape.

5. Inflation-Protected Model: 50% Equities, 25% Gold, 25% Real Estate

Given the potential for inflation and currency depreciation in India, an inflation-protected model focuses on assets that hold value over time. This model allocates

50% to equities for growth, 25% to gold for its inflation-hedging qualities, and 25% to real estate, another asset class that typically appreciates during inflationary periods.

This model leverages gold's intrinsic value and its ability to counterbalance inflation, while real estate provides long-term capital appreciation and protection against inflationary pressures. Equities capture market growth, making this model suitable for investors with a moderate risk tolerance who seek growth while prioritizing wealth preservation against inflation. This model works well for investors with a long-term horizon who can weather real estate market cycles and benefit from property value appreciation.

6. Aggressive Wealth Creation Model: 90% Equities, 10% Gold

This model is designed for young investors or those with a high-risk tolerance aiming for substantial wealth creation over a long period. A 90% allocation to equities allows investors to harness the full potential of stock market returns, capitalizing on high-growth sectors and emerging opportunities in the Indian economy. This aggressive model is well-suited to those with a horizon of 15 years or more, as equities tend to outperform other asset classes over extended periods.

The 10% allocation to gold provides minimal but essential protection against market shocks and inflation, adding a layer of stability to an otherwise aggressive portfolio. While this model offers high growth potential, it also requires a strong tolerance for risk and the discipline to stay invested through market cycles.

The tricky part: Selecting the Right Model

First things first, what is your goal? what you want to achieve from your investment?

For Indian investors, selecting an asset allocation model depends on personal risk tolerance, investment horizon, financial goals, and macroeconomic factors. Blending growth-oriented equities with stabilizing assets like gold allows for optimal diversification, creating a portfolio that can perform well in various market conditions. By choosing an asset allocation model aligned with their goals and adapting as necessary, investors can create a resilient strategy for both wealth accumulation and preservation.

Once you decide on the factors above, you will most likely be able to either choose an investment model or create your own unique one while starting your investment journey.

In this book, *Gold vs. the Indian Stock Market: History and the Way Forward*, we explore these asset allocation strategies in greater detail, offering guidance on how Indian investors can balance equities and gold to build a portfolio that is both adaptive and future-ready. Each model exemplifies the unique advantages of blending gold and equities, showcasing the importance of a well-constructed asset allocation in securing long-term financial success.

Case Studies on Portfolio Performance

Here lets see some case studies which will help us understand few investment models.

"Case Study 1: Growth-Oriented Portfolio During Economic Boom (2014-2018)"

From 2014 to 2018, India experienced a period of economic growth, fueled by policy reforms, increased foreign investments, and a bullish stock market. An 80% equity and 20% gold portfolio was particularly effective during this period. The BSE Sensex saw an annualized growth rate of over 10%, driven by robust performances in sectors like technology and financial services (National Stock Exchange of India, 2019). With 80% of the portfolio in equities, this allocation allowed investors to capitalize on high returns from the Indian stock market. The 20% allocation to gold added a layer of security without significantly diluting the growth potential, as gold's performance remained steady with moderate appreciation.

However, toward the end of 2018, volatility started to increase due to global trade tensions and inflationary pressures, and the gold allocation began to buffer the portfolio against equity downturns. This case demonstrates how a growth-oriented allocation benefits from strong economic conditions while maintaining resilience against unexpected fluctuations.

Reference: National Stock Exchange of India. (2019). Annual report 2018-2019. Retrieved from https://www.nseindia.com

Case Study 2: Balanced Portfolio During the COVID-19 Crisis (2020)

The COVID-19 pandemic in 2020 created unprecedented disruptions in the global economy, leading to severe volatility in the Indian stock market. In this context, a balanced portfolio of 60% equities, 30% fixed income, and 10% gold demonstrated resilience. The equity portion faced a sharp decline of approximately 30% in March 2020 due to widespread market panic (Bombay Stock Exchange, 2021). However, gold prices surged by 28% during the same year as investors sought stability in safe-hold assets, which mitigated the losses from equities.

By year-end, this balanced portfolio had rebounded, with the gold allocation offsetting much of the equity decline, enabling the portfolio to recover quicker than an all-equity portfolio. This case exemplifies the value of a diversified approach during crises, illustrating how gold's countercyclical behavior can support portfolio stability in the face of economic shocks.

Reference: Bombay Stock Exchange. (2021). Market trends and impact of COVID-19. Retrieved from https://www.bseindia.com

"Case Study 3: Conservative Portfolio in a High Inflation Environment (2021-2022)"

Between 2021 and 2022, inflation rose globally, impacting the purchasing power of investors and causing market volatility as central banks raised interest rates. An Indian investor with a conservative portfolio comprising 40% equities, 40% fixed income, and 20% gold witnessed notable protection against inflationary pressures. The equity portion faced instability due to the Reserve Bank of India's rate hikes aimed at curbing inflation, which affected corporate borrowing costs and reduced profit margins (Reserve Bank of India, 2022). However, the gold allocation appreciated as it gained value in response to inflation and rupee depreciation, particularly as global demand for gold increased.

This conservative portfolio minimized losses compared to equity-heavy portfolios and preserved capital, underscoring the importance of gold's inflation-hedging properties. The increased allocation to fixed income also provided a predictable income stream, proving advantageous in a high-inflation environment where equities were under pressure.

Reference: Reserve Bank of India. (2022). Annual report 2021-2022. Retrieved from https://www.rbi.org.in

"*Case Study 4: Adaptive Portfolio Model During the Russia-Ukraine Conflict (2022)*"

The Russia-Ukraine conflict in 2022 sparked global economic instability, supply chain disruptions, and surging energy prices, which had an immediate effect on Indian equities and currency values. An adaptive portfolio model—shifting from 70% equities and 20% gold pre-conflict to 50% equities, 30% gold, and 20% fixed income post-conflict—proved effective. Initially, the portfolio benefited from a high equity allocation, but as tensions escalated and stock markets declined, the increased allocation to gold and fixed income buffered losses (World Gold Council, 2022).

This shift reflected the importance of dynamically adjusting asset allocation to respond to geopolitical risks and volatility. As gold's price rose due to the increased demand for defensive assets, the portfolio outperformed a static allocation, showing that an adaptive approach can safeguard returns when market conditions shift rapidly.

Reference: World Gold Council. (2022). Gold demand trends Q1 2022. Retrieved from https://www.gold.org

Insights from the cases

These case studies illustrate the effectiveness of various asset allocation models under differing economic conditions, highlighting the unique benefits of combining gold with equities in a portfolio. During periods of economic expansion, a growth-oriented model maximizes returns, whereas a balanced or conservative model provides stability during crises and inflationary periods. The adaptive model underscores the value of flexibility, allowing investors to protect their portfolios from geopolitical risks and economic downturns by adjusting their allocations to suit changing conditions.

Through these cases, Indian investors can see the tangible benefits of diversification, particularly in incorporating gold as a buffer against volatility. These real-world examples underscore the themes discussed in Gold vs. the Indian Stock Market: History and the Way Forward, providing actionable insights into asset allocation strategies that offer both growth and resilience.

CHAPTER EIGHT

Choosing Between Gold and Stocks: Key Considerations

Investment Goals and Time Horizons

When choosing between gold and stocks, Indian investors must consider their specific investment goals and time horizons, as these factors significantly influence the appropriate asset allocation strategy. While both gold and equities play vital roles in a diversified portfolio, they serve distinct functions based on their risk profiles, growth potential, and ability to preserve wealth. Understanding how these factors align with individual investment objectives and timelines helps investors make informed decisions that enhance portfolio resilience and return potential.

Investment Goals: Growth vs. Preservation

For investors focused on capital growth, equities are often better suitable for investors seeking capital growth due to their potential for high long-term returns. Stocks indicate ownership in a company, allowing investors to share in corporate profits and the overall economic growth. As India's economy expands, equities in high-growth sectors like technology, healthcare, and consumer goods provide many potential for wealth building. However, equities are more volatile and sensitive to economic cycles, which can lead to significant declines. For growth-oriented investors, particularly those with a long-term vision, an equity-heavy allocation is consistent with the goal of wealth building, as equities have historically outperformed other asset classes over extended periods of time.

Gold is a wise investment option for anyone looking to preserve their riches. Gold is prized for its stability and intrinsic value, which serve as a buffer against inflation, currency depreciation, and economic instability. For example, during the 2008 financial crisis and the 2020 COVID-19 pandemic, gold prices rose as investors sought a safe-haven asset that holds its value when markets are volatile. Thus, investors that value stability and protection against negative risks benefit from a higher gold allocation, which balances portfolio volatility and protects purchasing power, particularly during economic downturns.

Time Horizons: Long-Term vs. Short-Term Investments

An investor's time horizon is crucial in determining the balance between gold and stocks. Long-term investors, generally those with an investment horizon of 10 years or more, have the capacity to withstand short-term volatility, making equities a favorable choice. Stocks provide the compounding advantage, where reinvested dividends and capital gains accumulate significantly over time. For instance, historical data on the BSE Sensex shows that equities have consistently delivered high returns over long periods, despite interim fluctuations. A long-term horizon allows investors to ride out market cycles, recovering from downturns and capitalizing on sustained economic growth.

For short-term investors,

typically with a horizon of fewer than five years, gold becomes an attractive option due to its stability and liquidity. Short-term market fluctuations can significantly impact stock returns, leading to potential capital loss if investors need to withdraw during a downturn. Gold, in contrast, has shown resilience and often performs well during market downturns, providing a more reliable store of value. This makes gold suitable for short-term investors looking to protect capital from immediate risks, such as currency depreciation and inflation

Blending Gold and Stocks for Different Investment Horizons

For investors with medium-term horizons (5-10 years),

a balanced approach that blends equities and gold can be highly effective. A portfolio with 60% equities and 40% gold, for example, allows investors to capture growth while managing risk. Equities in this model contribute to capital appreciation, while gold adds stability, protecting against mid-term market volatility. The balanced allocation aligns with the medium-term goal of achieving growth without excessive exposure to market downturns, making it ideal for investors with moderate risk tolerance.

Aligning Assets with Objectives

Choosing between gold and stocks is not an either-or decision but rather an exercise in aligning assets with investment goals and timelines. For Indian investors, equities offer high growth potential suited to long-term wealth-building objectives, while gold provides stability and wealth preservation, particularly valuable in short and uncertain investment periods. By understanding these distinctions, investors can tailor their portfolios to achieve optimal outcomes, balancing growth and stability in a way that aligns with their unique financial goals and time horizons.

In *Gold vs. the Indian Stock Market: History and the Way Forward*, these considerations are further explored to equip readers with strategies that address diverse investment needs. A nuanced approach to asset allocation—recognizing when to favour gold, equities, or a balanced mix—ensures that portfolios remain resilient and productive, regardless of economic conditions.

Risk Appetite and Economic Conditions

The interplay between an investor's risk appetite and prevailing economic conditions is pivotal when determining the optimal balance between gold and equities in a portfolio. Risk appetite—essentially, an investor's willingness to accept potential losses in pursuit of returns—varies significantly based on individual circumstances and economic outlooks. In the context of Indian investors navigating the complexities of economic cycles, inflationary pressures, and geopolitical uncertainties, choosing the right allocation between equities and gold requires a nuanced understanding of both risk tolerance and macroeconomic conditions.

Understanding Risk Appetite: Conservative vs. Aggressive Investors

Investors with a conservative risk appetite prioritize capital preservation over high returns. Their main goal is to protect their wealth against market volatility and economic downturns, making them more inclined towards assets with lower risk profiles, such as gold. Gold's intrinsic value, low correlation with equities, and historical performance during crises make it an appealing choice for conservative investors. For example, during the 2008 financial crisis and the 2020 COVID-19 pandemic, gold appreciated significantly as equities plummeted, providing a cushion against extreme market losses. Consequently, conservative investors often allocate a higher proportion of their portfolio to gold, using it as a hedge against the uncertainties of the stock market.

On the other hand, aggressive investors are more willing to accept short-term volatility for the prospect of long-term capital appreciation. Equities offer the growth potential that aligns with this approach, as they can deliver substantial returns during periods of economic expansion. For instance, the BSE Sensex has historically generated strong returns during bullish cycles, driven by sectors such as technology, financials, and consumer goods. Aggressive investors tend to favor equities for their ability to compound wealth over time, but they should remain mindful of the risks associated with market downturns, inflation, and currency fluctuations that can adversely impact returns.

Economic Conditions: Expansions, Recessions, and Inflationary Cycles

Economic conditions play a crucial role in influencing the performance of gold and equities, as well as investors' risk appetite. In expansive economic cycles, characterized by GDP growth, low inflation, and rising corporate earnings, equities tend to outperform gold. Companies benefit from increased consumer spending and business investments, translating into higher stock prices. During these periods, an equity-heavy portfolio can maximize growth opportunities, making it suitable for investors with a higher risk tolerance and a long-term outlook.

Conversely, during economic recessions or periods of contraction, equities become vulnerable to declining profits, reduced consumer spending, and market volatility. For example, during the COVID-19 pandemic, equities faced a sharp downturn due to lockdowns and disrupted economic activity. In such scenarios, gold tends to perform well, as investors seek a stable asset that can preserve wealth. Gold's appeal increases during market downturns, reflecting its role as a defensive asset that can offset losses in riskier investments. For Indian investors, adding gold during recessionary periods can mitigate the impact of stock market declines and enhance portfolio stability.

During inflationary cycles, gold becomes an essential asset due to its ability to act as a hedge against the eroding purchasing power of fiat currencies. As inflation rises, the value of currency decreases, and the real returns on fixed-income and equity investments diminish. Gold, however, often appreciates in response to inflationary pressures, as seen in 2021-2022, when global inflation led to a surge in gold prices. This makes gold a valuable component of a portfolio during inflationary periods, providing a buffer against the negative effects of rising prices and protecting the real value of wealth.

Matching Risk Appetite with Economic Conditions

Investors must tailor their portfolios to align with their risk tolerance and adapt to shifting economic conditions. In a booming economy, those with a higher risk appetite may prefer to overweight equities, taking advantage of growth sectors that deliver strong returns. However, a prudent strategy would still include a portion of gold, serving as a safeguard against unforeseen market disruptions.

During periods of economic uncertainty or recession, conservative investors may shift towards a higher allocation of gold, reducing their exposure to volatile equities. This approach offers protection against downside risk while preserving capital. For aggressive investors, maintaining a diversified approach that includes some allocation to gold can help balance risk without sacrificing the potential for recovery-driven gains in equities.

The adaptive portfolio strategy is an ideal approach for managing varying risk appetites and economic conditions. By dynamically adjusting allocations—such as increasing gold exposure during downturns and boosting equity allocation during economic recoveries—investors can optimize their portfolios for both resilience and growth. This strategy requires active management and regular rebalancing, but it provides the flexibility needed to navigate changing economic landscapes effectively.

A Strategic Balance for Long-Term Success

Balancing risk appetite with economic conditions is essential for building a robust portfolio that can withstand volatility while pursuing long-term growth. Indian investors face unique challenges, including currency fluctuations, inflation, and sensitivity to global economic cycles. By understanding their risk tolerance and responding to economic shifts with a flexible asset allocation strategy, they can achieve a balanced portfolio that is resilient, adaptable, and aligned with their financial objectives. Incorporating both equities and gold, tailored to prevailing economic conditions and individual risk profiles, allows for a sophisticated investment strategy that ensures long-term financial security.

Gold vs. the Indian Stock Market: History and the Way Forward delves deeper into these considerations, offering strategic guidance on how to navigate the complexities of asset allocation. By recognizing the critical role that risk appetite and economic conditions play in shaping investment decisions, investors can approach their portfolios with confidence and clarity, positioning themselves for success across different market cycles.

Factors Favouring Gold vs. Factors Favouring Equities

In constructing a balanced and resilient portfolio, Indian investors often weigh the benefits of holding gold versus equities. Each asset class offers distinct advantages, shaped by market conditions, economic trends, and investment objectives. Gold and equities respond differently to inflation, currency fluctuations, and economic growth cycles, which makes understanding their unique benefits essential for strategic asset allocation. Here, we explore the factors favoring gold and equities, providing a comparative analysis that highlights when each asset class may be preferable.

Factors Favoring Gold
Inflation Hedge
Gold is a well-established hedge against inflation, appreciated for its ability to retain value even when fiat

currencies lose purchasing power. During inflationary periods, gold typically performs well as investors seek refuge in assets with intrinsic value. This was particularly evident in 2021-2022, when global inflation led to a significant rise in gold prices, helping investors preserve wealth in the face of rising prices.

Safe-Hold Asset During Economic Uncertainty

Gold's appeal is amplified during economic downturns, market crises, and geopolitical instability. For example, during the 2008 financial crisis and the COVID-19 pandemic, gold prices surged as investors moved away from riskier assets like stocks. Gold's counter-cyclical nature makes it a stabilizing force in portfolios, especially during periods of extreme market volatility or uncertainty.

Protection Against Currency Depreciation

In emerging economies like India, where the currency is more prone to depreciation against global currencies like the U.S. dollar, gold provides a reliable safeguard. When the rupee weakens, the price of gold in INR terms often rises, preserving purchasing power for Indian investors. This dynamic makes gold an attractive option for those concerned about currency risk and its impact on domestic investments.

Low Correlation with Equities

Gold exhibits a low or negative correlation with equities, which enhances its value in a diversified portfolio. When stock markets face downturns, gold often performs well, providing a hedge against losses in other asset classes. This characteristic allows gold to reduce overall portfolio volatility, making it a preferred asset for risk-averse investors seeking stability alongside growth-oriented assets.

Tangible Asset with Historical Value

As a tangible asset, gold has inherent value that is unaffected by corporate earnings, monetary policy, or credit risk. This attribute has sustained its appeal over centuries as a reliable store of value. Unlike equities, which can fluctuate based on company-specific factors, gold provides a consistent value base, making it a conservative choice for investors looking to preserve wealth over long periods.

Factors Favoring Equities

Growth Potential and Capital Appreciation

Equities offer unparalleled potential for capital growth, especially in high-growth economies like India. By investing in stocks, investors can benefit from corporate profitability, economic expansion, and market growth. For example, the BSE Sensex has delivered substantial returns over the long term, reflecting the overall growth trajectory of the Indian economy. For investors focused on wealth accumulation, equities provide a higher growth rate compared to gold, which relies primarily on price appreciation rather than compounding gains from business growth.

Dividend Income and Compounding Benefits

Many equities pay dividends, providing investors with a source of regular income in addition to capital gains. Dividend-paying stocks contribute to portfolio returns, especially when dividends are reinvested, compounding growth over time. This attribute makes equities attractive for investors with a long-term horizon, as reinvested dividends can significantly boost portfolio value, creating compounded returns that gold cannot match.

Economic Growth Correlation

Equities are directly tied to economic growth, benefiting

from increases in consumer spending, corporate investments, and government policies that support business expansion. During periods of economic prosperity, companies generate higher profits, leading to rising stock prices. For Indian investors, equities allow participation in sectors driving economic growth, such as technology, financial services, and consumer goods, providing exposure to the upward trends in the economy.

Liquidity and Accessibility

Equities offer a high degree of liquidity, allowing investors to buy or sell shares relatively easily. The stock market's accessibility through online trading platforms has made equities a convenient investment vehicle for a wide range of investors. Unlike gold, which may involve storage costs or require physical ownership, equities can be bought and sold instantly, making them ideal for investors seeking flexibility and easy access to their capital.

Portfolio Diversification with Sectoral Exposure

Investing in equities provides diversification opportunities across various sectors, allowing investors to allocate capital in industries with differing growth drivers and risk profiles. By spreading investments across sectors such as healthcare, finance, energy, and consumer technology, investors can mitigate sector-specific risks and enhance portfolio resilience. This sectoral diversification is unique to equities, as gold remains a single-asset class without exposure to the nuances of different industries.

When to love Gold vs. Equities

The decision to favor gold or equities depends largely on market conditions, economic forecasts, and individual investment goals. In times of economic expansion and low inflation, equities tend to outperform due to their growth potential and correlation with corporate earnings.

However, during periods of economic recession, high inflation, or geopolitical instability, gold provides valuable protection as it holds or appreciates in value while equities may decline.

For Indian investors, balancing these assets based on economic indicators is essential. For example, during periods of rupee depreciation or rising inflation, gold can act as a defensive asset, shielding portfolios from the adverse effects of currency and inflationary pressures. On the other hand, when market sentiment is optimistic and economic growth is accelerating, an equity-heavy allocation allows investors to benefit from higher returns.

In Gold vs. the Indian Stock Market: History and the Way Forward, we further explore how investors can harness the strengths of both asset classes, offering practical insights into asset allocation strategies that optimize returns and safeguard against market risks. The dynamic balance between gold and equities creates a portfolio resilient to market cycles, positioning investors for long-term financial security.

CHAPTER NINE

Technological Impact on Investments in Gold and Stocks

Digital Gold Investments and Accessibility

The digital revolution has transformed the investment landscape for both gold and equities, making these assets more accessible, transparent, and efficient for Indian investors. Technological advancements in digital trading, online platforms, and mobile applications have significantly lowered barriers to entry, enabling more investors to participate in the markets with ease. This shift has also introduced innovative avenues such as digital gold investments, enhancing accessibility and convenience. Understanding the impact of technology on gold and stock investments sheds light on how these innovations are shaping portfolio management, wealth-building strategies, and investor behavior.

Digital Gold Investments: Accessibility and Flexibility

Digital gold has redefined how investors engage with gold, democratizing access to this precious metal and eliminating traditional barriers like storage concerns and high initial costs. In a digital gold investment, investors can purchase fractional amounts of gold online, which is securely stored by third-party providers in insured vaults. This innovation allows investors to acquire gold in small amounts, as low as one rupee, making it possible for individuals to build their gold holdings incrementally, regardless of budget constraints. Companies such as MMTC-PAMP, SafeGold, and various mobile payment platforms like Paytm and PhonePe have popularized digital gold in India, offering secure, easy-to-use platforms for transactions.

The accessibility provided by digital gold is especially appealing to younger, tech-savvy investors who may not have the capital for large physical gold purchases but still want to diversify their portfolios. Digital gold can be bought and sold 24/7, allowing investors to manage their gold holdings with the same flexibility as equities. This convenience has made gold more accessible than ever, expanding its role beyond a traditional store of value to a flexible, digitally integrated asset.

Moreover, digital gold investments allow for seamless redemption options, where investors can choose to convert their digital holdings into physical gold, typically in the form of coins or bars, delivered directly to their doorstep. This feature combines the benefits of physical ownership with the convenience of digital transactions, appealing to investors who value the tangible aspect of gold but prefer a modern approach to acquisition and storage.

Increased Participation in Equity Markets Through Digital Platforms

Technology has also revolutionized the way investors interact with the stock market. Online brokerage platforms, mobile trading apps, and robo-advisors have streamlined the process of buying and selling stocks, making equities more accessible to a broader demographic. Platforms such as Zerodha, Upstox, and Groww have simplified trading by offering user-friendly interfaces, low or zero brokerage fees, and educational resources to empower first-time investors. As a result, India has witnessed a sharp increase in retail participation in the stock market, with the number of Demat accounts surpassing 100 million by 2023.

This surge in retail investor participation is partly attributed to the convenience of digital platforms, which allow investors to trade and manage portfolios on their smartphones. Mobile trading apps provide real-time data, financial news, analytical tools, and portfolio tracking features, enabling investors to make informed decisions from anywhere. This accessibility has bridged the gap between institutional and retail investors, allowing individuals to take advantage of market opportunities with greater ease.

Additionally, digital equity platforms have introduced innovative tools such as algorithm-based portfolio management, customizable investment strategies, and systematic investment plans (SIPs), making it easier for investors to implement disciplined, long-term strategies. These features democratize access to professional-grade investment tools, empowering retail investors to engage with equities more confidently.

Transparency and Security Through Blockchain and Digital Verification

One of the most significant technological advancements affecting both digital gold and equities is blockchain technology. Blockchain enables secure, transparent transactions by recording ownership and transfers on a distributed ledger, minimizing fraud and enhancing security. In the context of digital gold, blockchain technology verifies authenticity and ownership, providing investors with confidence in the quality and legitimacy of their holdings.

In the equities market, blockchain has the potential to streamline processes such as settlement, clearing, and compliance, making transactions faster and more efficient. Some digital platforms are already experimenting with blockchain-based systems to facilitate instant settlement of trades, reduce administrative costs, and improve transparency in regulatory compliance. These advancements benefit both retail and institutional investors, as they reduce transaction costs and increase trust in the investment process.

Impact on Portfolio Diversification and Strategy

The rise of digital platforms for gold and equity investments has made it easier for investors to diversify their portfolios, offering the flexibility to allocate funds across various asset classes with minimal friction. Digital platforms provide seamless access to gold, stocks, bonds, mutual funds, and even alternative assets, enabling investors to tailor portfolios according to their risk tolerance, financial goals, and economic outlooks. This ease of diversification is particularly valuable in volatile markets, where balanced exposure to different assets helps reduce risk.

For instance, an investor might allocate a portion of their portfolio to digital gold as a hedge against inflation and currency depreciation, while using an online trading app to build an equity portfolio focused on growth sectors like technology and consumer goods. This flexibility allows investors to manage their allocations dynamically, adapting to changing economic conditions in real time.

A New Era of Accessible, Tech-Enabled Investments

Technology has undeniably transformed the investment landscape for gold and stocks, offering Indian investors unprecedented levels of accessibility, transparency, and control. Digital gold platforms enable fractional ownership, eliminating storage and liquidity concerns, and making gold a more versatile asset. Meanwhile, mobile trading apps and online brokerage platforms have democratized access to equities, fostering a new generation of retail investors who can participate actively in the market.

In Gold vs. the Indian Stock Market: History and the Way Forward, we examine the implications of these technological advancements on investment strategies, highlighting how digital platforms are shaping the future of wealth management. With technology at the forefront, investors are better equipped to harness the strengths of both gold and equities, building resilient portfolios that can withstand market volatility and capitalize on opportunities for growth.

The Rise of Online Trading

The advent of online trading has revolutionized the financial landscape, transforming how investors engage with the stock market. For Indian investors, in particular, online trading platforms have democratized access to equities, providing convenience, affordability, and an unprecedented level of control over personal investments.

Over the past decade, online trading has become increasingly popular, driven by technological advancements, the proliferation of mobile applications, and a shift toward digital financial literacy. This rise has not only expanded retail investor participation but also reshaped the structure of India's stock market.

Accessibility and Convenience

One of the most significant impacts of online trading is its accessibility. Platforms such as Zerodha, Upstox, Groww, and Angel Broking have simplified the process of opening a Demat account, enabling investors to start trading with just a smartphone and internet connection. The traditional barriers to entry—such as high brokerage fees, extensive paperwork, and the need for in-person interactions with brokers—have been dismantled. Today, investors can initiate trades in seconds, access real-time data, and monitor portfolios on the go. The ability to trade 24/7 (in the case of global markets) and access detailed market insights has made investing more approachable for individuals who might not have considered it before.

This convenience has significantly increased retail participation in the stock market. By 2023, the number of Demat accounts in India exceeded 100 million, reflecting a sharp rise in individual investors eager to participate in wealth creation. The accessibility of online trading has also encouraged younger investors, many of whom are more comfortable with digital technology, to enter the market.

Lower Costs and Transparent Pricing

Online trading platforms have introduced a competitive pricing structure, significantly reducing or even eliminating brokerage fees. Discount brokers, such as Zerodha and Upstox, have adopted zero-commission or flat-fee models, allowing investors to trade with minimal costs. This shift has made investing affordable, especially for those with smaller portfolios, and has increased transparency, as investors can see exactly what they are paying for each transaction.

Low fees are particularly beneficial for high-frequency traders, who can now execute multiple trades without incurring high brokerage charges. In addition, online trading platforms provide users with access to various financial products, including equities, mutual funds, exchange-traded funds (ETFs), and even digital gold, all from a single account. This cost efficiency has empowered more individuals to engage in regular, active trading, which was previously viable only for those with larger capital.

Educational Resources and Market Insights

The rise of online trading has been accompanied by a surge in digital financial literacy. Most online trading platforms offer educational resources such as webinars, tutorials, and market insights to help novice investors make informed decisions. Platforms like Groww and Zerodha's Varsity provide comprehensive learning modules that cover topics ranging from basic stock market concepts to advanced trading strategies. By fostering a culture of financial literacy, these platforms empower retail investors to navigate the complexities of investing independently.

In addition, online trading platforms offer in-depth analysis, stock screeners, news updates, and technical indicators, giving users the tools to conduct their research. This abundance of information enables investors to assess market conditions, track economic trends, and build more informed portfolios. The availability of such resources has shifted the market from a reliance on brokerage recommendations toward more self-directed investing, as individuals gain confidence in making their investment choices.

Real-Time Trading and Decision-Making

In traditional trading, delays in executing orders could lead to missed opportunities or changes in market prices by the time trades were completed. Online trading platforms have eliminated these delays by enabling real-time trading, where investors can execute orders instantly. This feature is crucial in today's fast-paced markets, where prices fluctuate rapidly, and timely decisions can be the difference between profit and loss.

Real-time trading also allows investors to react swiftly to news and events impacting the market. For example, earnings announcements, geopolitical events, or changes in government policies can lead to significant market shifts. Online platforms' instant trading capabilities enable investors to adjust their positions immediately in response to such developments, providing them with a strategic advantage.

Rise of Algorithmic and Automated Trading

Algorithmic and automated trading have become integral to online trading platforms, allowing retail investors to employ sophisticated trading strategies without extensive manual effort. With algorithmic trading, users can set specific parameters—such as price points, stop losses, and profit targets—and have trades executed automatically based on these predefined criteria. This automation minimizes emotional decision-making and ensures disciplined, consistent trading strategies.

Robo-advisors, another product of technological advancement, offer automated portfolio management services tailored to individual risk tolerance, financial goals, and time horizons. These robo-advisors use algorithms to recommend a diversified mix of assets, periodically rebalance portfolios, and reinvest dividends, making them ideal for investors who prefer a passive approach. Platforms like ET Money, Scripbox, and Paytm Money have introduced robo-advisory features, making personalized, data-driven portfolio management accessible to the average investor.

Increased Retail Influence on Market Dynamics

The rise of online trading has shifted the dynamics of India's stock market, with retail investors playing an increasingly prominent role. Traditionally, institutional investors like mutual funds and foreign institutional investors (FIIs) dominated trading volumes, dictating market trends and liquidity. However, the influx of retail investors through online platforms has brought a new wave of capital and participation to the market. The influence of retail investors was particularly evident during the COVID-19 pandemic when stock markets recovered from initial declines with strong retail participation, even as institutional flows remained cautious.

This democratization of market influence has led to new trends and behaviors, as retail investors increasingly pursue diversified portfolios that include not only large-cap stocks but also small and mid-cap stocks, which offer higher growth potential. Online forums, social media, and peer-to-peer learning have further fueled retail enthusiasm, enabling individual investors to collectively influence stock trends.

A Paradigm Shift in Investing

The rise of online trading marks a paradigm shift in how Indian investors approach the stock market, democratizing access and empowering individuals to take control of their financial futures. Through enhanced accessibility, cost efficiency, educational resources, real-time trading, and automated strategies, online platforms have broken down barriers, making it easier than ever for individuals to invest. This technological advancement has not only expanded market participation but also created a more inclusive financial ecosystem where retail investors can play an active and influential role.

Future Trends in Gold and Stock Market Technology

Artificial Intelligence and Machine Learning

Artificial Intelligence (AI) and Machine Learning (ML) are increasingly being integrated into investment strategies. These technologies analyze vast datasets to identify patterns, forecast market trends, and optimize portfolios. For instance, AI-driven robo-advisors offer personalized investment advice and automated portfolio management, making sophisticated financial planning accessible to retail investors. In the stock market, AI algorithms are employed for high-frequency trading, risk assessment, and fraud detection, enhancing market efficiency and security.

Decentralized Finance (DeFi) Platforms

Decentralized Finance platforms are emerging as alternatives to traditional financial systems, offering services such as lending, borrowing, and trading without intermediaries. In the context of gold, DeFi platforms enable users to trade tokenized gold assets, providing liquidity and flexibility. Similarly, DeFi applications in the stock market allow for peer-to-peer trading of tokenized securities, potentially reducing reliance on traditional exchanges and brokers. However, DeFi platforms also pose regulatory challenges and risks related to security and market volatility.

Integration of Internet of Things (IoT) in Gold Supply Chain

The Internet of Things is being integrated into the gold supply chain to enhance transparency and traceability. IoT devices can monitor the movement and condition of gold from mining to storage, ensuring authenticity and ethical sourcing. This technology addresses concerns about conflict minerals and environmental impact, providing consumers and investors with verifiable information about the origin and journey of their gold investments.

Technological advancements are reshaping the investment landscape for gold and the stock market, offering enhanced accessibility, efficiency, and transparency. Investors must stay informed about these developments to leverage new opportunities and navigate associated risks effectively. As technology continues to evolve, it will play a pivotal role in defining the future dynamics of gold and stock market investments.

The Way Forward

CHAPTER TEN

Future Outlook for Gold and Indian Equities

Economic and Market Forecasts

The future outlook for gold and Indian equities is shaped by global economic dynamics, monetary policies, and domestic growth projections. For Indian investors, understanding these trends and aligning them with their investment strategies is essential, particularly in a market that faces both promising growth prospects and complex economic challenges. By examining the factors influencing the outlook for gold and equities, investors can make informed decisions that balance potential for growth with the stability offered by gold.

Gold Market Outlook

Gold has reached near-record highs in recent months, fueled by escalating geopolitical uncertainties, economic shifts, and monetary policy adjustments. As of late 2024, spot gold prices rose above $2,780 per ounce, bolstered by increased investor demand for safe-haven assets amid a volatile global backdrop. The uncertainty surrounding geopolitical tensions, central bank interventions, and inflationary pressures have heightened demand for gold, driving prices to levels not seen in recent years.

Looking ahead, Goldman Sachs projects that gold prices could climb even further, potentially reaching $2,900 per ounce by early 2025. This forecast is influenced by several key factors:

Central Bank Purchases: Many central banks, particularly in emerging economies, have been increasing their gold reserves to diversify their portfolios away from the U.S. dollar. This trend is expected to continue, sustaining demand for gold and supporting price increases.

Geopolitical Uncertainty: Geopolitical events, such as the ongoing conflicts in Europe and Middle Eastern tensions, contribute to gold's appeal as a safe-haven asset. In times of heightened global risk, investors typically turn to gold as a wealth preservation strategy.

Interest Rate Policies: Speculation around potential interest rate cuts in major economies, including the United States, could make gold more attractive by reducing the opportunity cost of holding non-yielding assets like gold.

For Indian investors, these trends underscore the importance of considering gold as a stable, wealth-preserving component in a diversified portfolio. As the rupee may experience periods of volatility due to external pressures and fluctuating global markets, gold offers a hedge against currency depreciation and provides a store of value in times of economic stress.

Indian Equities Outlook

India's economy is expected to grow at a steady pace, driven by robust domestic demand, structural reforms, and government initiatives. The International Monetary Fund (IMF) has retained its optimistic forecast for India, projecting a GDP growth rate of 7% for the fiscal year 2024-2025, followed by 6.5% growth in 2025-2026. This growth outlook is promising for Indian equities, which are likely to benefit from an expanding economy, higher corporate earnings, and the ongoing development of critical sectors such as technology, financial services, and infrastructure.

However, there are a few key challenges and considerations for Indian equities:

Inflationary Pressures: Although inflation is expected to moderate in the near term, persistent inflationary pressures could impact consumer spending and corporate profits. The Reserve Bank of India (RBI) has been closely monitoring inflation trends and is considering a potential rate cut of 25 basis points by December to support economic growth.

Job Creation and Employment Rates: Moderate job growth remains a concern in India, particularly in the informal sector. Although GDP growth is robust, achieving inclusive growth will require strong employment numbers, which directly influence consumer spending and economic resilience.

Global Economic Slowdown: Indian equities may face external pressures from a potential global economic slowdown. The Indian stock market is integrated with global markets, meaning that disruptions in major economies like the U.S. and the EU can impact foreign investment flows and investor sentiment in India.

Despite these challenges, sectors like renewable energy, digital technology, and manufacturing (especially in the context of India's "Make in India" initiative) are expected to drive long-term growth in the Indian stock market. For investors with a growth-oriented risk appetite, Indian equities offer substantial potential for capital appreciation, especially as the country remains one of the fastest-growing major economies globally.

Strategic Positioning in a Dynamic Economic Landscape

The future outlook for gold and Indian equities highlights the necessity of a diversified investment strategy. For Indian investors, economic expansion offers opportunities for growth in equities, while gold serves as a reliable hedge against unforeseen economic shocks and market volatility. In this context, balancing exposure to both asset classes allows for a portfolio that not only pursues growth but also preserves wealth during uncertain times.

Emerging Trends and Investment Products

The investment landscape is evolving with several emerging trends and innovative products that are reshaping portfolios and strategies. Investors are increasingly focusing on sustainable investments, technological advancements, and alternative assets to enhance returns and manage risks.

1. Sustainable and Green Investments

Environmental, Social, and Governance (ESG) criteria have become central to investment decisions. Investors are prioritizing companies with strong ESG practices, leading to the growth of green bonds and sustainable funds. This shift reflects a broader commitment to responsible investing and recognition of the long-term benefits of sustainability.

2. Technological Integration in Investment Platforms

The adoption of Artificial Intelligence (AI) and Machine Learning (ML) in investment platforms is enhancing decision-making processes. These technologies analyze vast datasets to identify patterns and forecast market trends, enabling more informed and timely investment decisions. Additionally, blockchain technology is being utilized for asset tokenization, increasing liquidity and accessibility.

3. Rise of Decentralized Finance (DeFi)

DeFi platforms are offering financial services without traditional intermediaries, providing opportunities for lending, borrowing, and trading in a decentralized environment. This trend is democratizing access to financial services and introducing new investment avenues, though it also presents regulatory and security challenges.

4. Growth of Private Credit Markets

Private credit funds are expanding, meeting the financing needs of businesses and offering investors higher yields compared to traditional fixed-income securities. This growth is driven by regulatory changes and the search for alternative income sources in a low-interest-rate environment.

5. Emphasis on Infrastructure Investments

Investments in infrastructure are gaining traction, supported by government initiatives and the need for modernization. These investments offer stable returns and are seen as essential for economic development, particularly in emerging markets.

6. Diversification into Emerging Markets

Investors are increasingly looking to emerging markets for diversification and growth opportunities. These markets offer potential for higher returns, though they come with increased volatility and geopolitical risks.

7. Adoption of Digital Gold Investments

Digital gold platforms are making gold investments more accessible, allowing fractional ownership and eliminating storage concerns. This innovation caters to a broader demographic, including younger investors seeking diversification.

These trends highlight a dynamic investment environment where technological advancements and a focus on sustainability are driving the development of new products and strategies. Investors are encouraged to stay informed and adapt to these changes to optimize their portfolios.

Predicting Gold's Role in a Changing Economy

Gold as an Inflation Hedge in a High-Inflation Environment

With inflationary pressures on the rise in recent years, gold's role as a hedge against inflation is once again in focus. Historically, gold has preserved purchasing power during periods of high inflation, as seen in the 1970s and more recently in 2021-2022, when global inflation surged. The price of gold often rises in response to inflation, as investors seek to protect their wealth from the eroding value of fiat currencies. This quality makes gold particularly attractive in economies facing currency depreciation and inflationary risks.

Looking forward, if inflationary pressures remain high, demand for gold as a wealth-preserving asset is likely to grow. With central banks in emerging markets increasing their gold reserves as a buffer against currency volatility, gold's position as a stable, inflation-hedged asset seems assured. In economies like India, where inflation and currency fluctuations are recurrent concerns, gold's role in protecting purchasing power remains critical for long-term financial security.

Gold as a Safe-Hold Asset Amid Economic Uncertainty

In times of economic or geopolitical uncertainty, gold consistently functions as a safe-hold asset, providing stability when other markets fluctuate. The COVID-19 pandemic underscored gold's importance as a safe-haven asset, as prices surged in response to global market instability. Similarly, ongoing geopolitical tensions, including conflicts and trade disputes, reinforce gold's role as an asset for managing risk.

As economic cycles become more unpredictable, with factors like global trade dynamics, interest rate policies, and geopolitical shifts influencing markets, gold's value as a hedge against instability will likely strengthen. Investors may increasingly turn to gold during periods of heightened uncertainty, seeking a safe-hold asset to mitigate risk within their portfolios.

Gold's Role in Portfolio Diversification with Digital Integration

The advent of digital gold investments is making gold more accessible to retail investors, expanding its role beyond traditional physical holdings. Through digital platforms, investors can purchase fractional amounts of gold online, eliminating storage and liquidity concerns. Digital gold investments also make it easier for investors to add gold to their portfolios, enabling smoother diversification across asset classes.

Additionally, innovations like blockchain technology are enhancing transparency in the gold market by tracking provenance and verifying authenticity. Blockchain-based gold tokens provide new ways to invest in gold while maintaining verifiable ownership. As these technologies continue to evolve, they are expected to enhance gold's attractiveness by making it more accessible, verifiable, and adaptable to digital portfolios.

Gold as a Hedge Against Currency Depreciation in Emerging Markets

For emerging economies, currency depreciation poses a significant threat to purchasing power. As currencies weaken, particularly against the U.S. dollar, gold's value in local terms often increases, providing a hedge against currency volatility. This dynamic is especially relevant in India, where the rupee is subject to fluctuations based on global economic factors, trade imbalances, and monetary policies.

With ongoing uncertainties surrounding major currencies, gold's role as a currency hedge remains essential for investors in emerging markets. Central banks in several emerging economies have increased their gold holdings to reduce reliance on foreign currencies, adding a layer of security to national reserves. For individual investors in these regions, holding gold acts as a safeguard against domestic currency depreciation, offering stability in the face of unpredictable currency shifts.

Gold as an Asset in Sustainable and Ethical Investing

With a growing emphasis on sustainable investing, the environmental and ethical aspects of gold are becoming increasingly significant. Responsible mining practices and ethical sourcing are essential to maintaining gold's appeal to environmentally conscious investors. The gold industry is responding by implementing standards for ethical sourcing, responsible mining, and reduced environmental impact.

Gold's durability, recyclability, and value retention align with the principles of sustainable investing, making it an asset that supports long-term value without excessive environmental degradation. As investor awareness of sustainability grows, gold's role as an ethical, durable asset may further strengthen, attracting investors who prioritize environmental and social governance (ESG) principles.

Central Banks and Gold Reserves: A Long-Term Strategy

Central banks continue to be major buyers of gold, viewing it as a safe asset for reserve diversification. In the past decade, central banks in countries like China, India, and Russia have increased their gold reserves, reducing reliance on the U.S. dollar and safeguarding against currency volatility. This trend reflects a strategic shift in how nations approach reserve management, particularly amid concerns over global financial stability and potential currency devaluation.

Looking ahead, central bank demand for gold is likely to remain robust as countries aim to diversify their reserves. This sustained institutional demand provides a solid foundation for gold prices, reinforcing its role as a long-term, stable asset. For individual investors, central bank purchases serve as a signal of gold's enduring value and reliability.

Digital Financial Platforms and the Democratization of Gold Investing

Technological advancements in financial platforms have democratized access to gold, allowing retail investors to add gold to their portfolios through fractional ownership and digital trading. Platforms such as MMTC-PAMP and SafeGold in India enable investors to purchase gold in small amounts, making it accessible to those with limited capital. These platforms also offer liquidity and ease of trade, allowing investors to buy or sell gold quickly without traditional barriers.

As digital gold investments continue to grow, they are likely to attract a new generation of investors who value flexibility and accessibility. This trend broadens gold's appeal, integrating it into mainstream digital finance and offering diverse options for incorporating gold into portfolios of varying sizes and objectives.

CHAPTER ELEVEN

Building a Balanced Investment Portfolio

Long-term Strategies for Indian Investors

For Indian investors, creating a balanced investment portfolio that aligns with long-term financial goals requires strategic allocation, an understanding of market cycles, and a clear view of risk tolerance. A balanced portfolio combines high-growth assets like equities with stable assets like gold, blending growth and preservation to enhance resilience. As India's economy continues to expand amid global uncertainties, long-term strategies that incorporate a mix of equities, gold, and other complementary assets can help investors weather volatility and capitalize on growth opportunities.

Establishing a Core Allocation: Equities for Growth

Equities should form a significant portion of a long-term portfolio, given their potential to deliver robust returns that outpace inflation and support wealth accumulation. Indian equities, especially in high-growth sectors like technology, finance, and consumer goods, offer substantial upside as India's economy is projected to grow at an annual rate of

6-7% over the coming years. For investors with a long-term horizon, equities offer compounding potential, allowing reinvested gains to accelerate portfolio growth.

When selecting equities, a diversified approach across large-cap, mid-cap, and small-cap stocks can help mitigate risk. Large-cap stocks provide stability and steady growth, mid-cap stocks offer a balance between stability and growth potential, and small-cap stocks, though more volatile, offer high growth prospects. Additionally, sectoral diversification is crucial, as it spreads exposure across various industries, reducing vulnerability to sector-specific downturns. For instance, while technology and finance may offer high growth, consumer staples and utilities provide stability during economic slowdowns.

Gold as a Stabilizing Force in Volatile Markets

Gold remains a critical component in a balanced portfolio for Indian investors, particularly as a hedge against inflation and currency depreciation. Gold's value typically rises during periods of economic uncertainty, inflationary cycles, and currency volatility—factors that are especially relevant in emerging markets like India. With the rupee subject to depreciation against stronger currencies and India's economy exposed to global inflationary trends, gold provides stability and protects purchasing power.

Digital gold platforms, such as those offered by MMTC-PAMP and SafeGold, have made gold more accessible, allowing investors to purchase fractional amounts. This convenience allows for a steady accumulation of gold over time, building wealth preservation without requiring large upfront capital. A 10-20% allocation to gold is generally recommended for conservative investors, while more aggressive investors might maintain a smaller allocation, ensuring their portfolios are equipped to handle periods of market downturns without sacrificing growth potential.

Fixed-Income Investments for Income Stability

Fixed-income assets, such as government bonds, corporate bonds, and fixed deposits, provide stable, predictable returns, acting as an anchor during volatile periods. In a balanced portfolio, fixed-income investments offer a counterbalance to the risks associated with equities, providing regular income that can be reinvested for compounding growth or used to offset equity market losses. Government bonds, particularly those issued by the Reserve Bank of India, are highly secure and offer fixed returns, making them ideal for risk-averse investors.

Indian investors can also consider bond funds, which invest in a mix of corporate and government bonds, to add diversity within the fixed-income allocation. These funds tend to offer a slightly higher yield than traditional fixed deposits, though they carry additional risks based on interest rate changes. For investors nearing retirement or those with moderate risk tolerance, fixed-income investments can comprise 30-40% of the portfolio, enhancing stability and income predictability.

Real Estate and Infrastructure Investments for Tangible Asset Exposure

Real estate has long been a popular investment choice in India, valued for its tangible nature, potential for capital appreciation, and rental income. While real estate typically requires substantial upfront capital, real estate investment trusts (REITs) offer a more accessible way to gain exposure. REITs pool funds to invest in income-generating properties, providing investors with a share of rental income and potential capital gains without the complexity of property management.

Infrastructure funds, which invest in sectors like energy, transportation, and utilities, are another option for investors looking for stable, long-term returns tied to the growth of essential services. These investments align with India's rapid urbanization and government initiatives like the National Infrastructure Pipeline, which seeks to modernize India's infrastructure. Real estate and infrastructure investments are typically suitable for investors with a longer horizon, as they provide gradual appreciation and income over time.

Embracing Technological Advancements: Digital Gold, Robo-Advisors, and Algorithmic Trading

Incorporating technology into investment strategies can help Indian investors streamline portfolio management, improve decision-making, and enhance diversification. Digital platforms have made assets like gold more accessible, while robo-advisors and algorithmic trading tools offer customized, data-driven portfolio management. Robo-advisors, for example, use algorithms to create and rebalance portfolios based on individual risk tolerance and goals, providing a low-cost, automated approach to investing.

Algorithmic trading, available through platforms like Zerodha and Upstox, allows investors to set predetermined criteria for trades, reducing emotional decision-making and enhancing consistency. These technologies democratize access to sophisticated investment strategies, previously limited to institutional investors, making it easier for individual investors to maintain a balanced, diversified portfolio.

Systematic Investment Plans (SIPs): A Disciplined Approach to Building Wealth

For Indian investors focused on long-term growth, systematic investment plans (SIPs) in mutual funds provide a disciplined approach to building wealth through equities and bonds. SIPs allow investors to invest a fixed amount regularly, often monthly, into a mutual fund, averaging out the purchase price over time and mitigating the impact of market volatility. This approach is particularly effective in a volatile market, as it encourages consistent investing without trying to time the market.

SIPs are well-suited to young investors or those with limited upfront capital, as they enable gradual wealth accumulation. Equity mutual funds provide exposure to a diverse basket of stocks, while debt mutual funds offer the stability of fixed-income instruments. By automating investments through SIPs, investors benefit from compounding over the long term, gradually building a balanced portfolio that grows in alignment with their financial goals.

Adjusting Allocation Based on Economic Conditions

A dynamic allocation strategy, where investors adjust their portfolio's equity and gold allocations in response to economic conditions, is essential for long-term resilience. For instance, during periods of economic growth and low inflation, investors might increase their equity allocation to capture market gains. However, in times of high inflation or geopolitical uncertainty, a higher allocation to gold and fixed income could enhance portfolio stability and reduce risk exposure.

Monitoring indicators such as GDP growth rates, inflation, and central bank interest rate policies enables investors to make informed adjustments that align with prevailing economic conditions. This adaptive approach allows for proactive adjustments rather than reactive responses, positioning the portfolio to optimize returns and minimize risk across economic cycles.

A Balanced Strategy for Long-Term Financial Security

For Indian investors, building a balanced investment portfolio that withstands economic shifts and market cycles is essential for long-term financial success. By strategically allocating assets among equities, gold, fixed income, and alternative investments, investors create a portfolio that supports growth and preserves wealth. Incorporating technological tools, such as robo-advisors and algorithmic trading, and adopting disciplined investing methods, like SIPs, further enhance portfolio resilience and efficiency.

In Gold vs. the Indian Stock Market: History and the Way Forward, we explore how these strategies can help Indian investors achieve a balanced portfolio that adapts to changing economic conditions. By aligning their portfolios with long-term financial goals and periodically adjusting allocations, investors can navigate uncertainties while capitalizing on growth, ensuring a secure financial future.

Dynamic Asset Allocation: Adjusting to Market Changes

Dynamic asset allocation is a strategic approach that involves regularly adjusting a portfolio's asset mix in response to changing market conditions, economic indicators, and an investor's evolving financial goals. Unlike static asset allocation, which keeps a fixed asset mix over time, dynamic allocation is flexible and proactive, allowing investors to capitalize on market opportunities while managing risks effectively. For Indian investors, where market conditions can fluctuate due to both domestic and global influences, a dynamic approach can enhance portfolio resilience and optimize returns.

The Rationale for Dynamic Asset Allocation

Dynamic asset allocation is rooted in the understanding that market cycles and economic conditions do not remain constant. Factors like GDP growth, inflation, interest rates, and geopolitical events all impact asset performance, often in unpredictable ways. In such a context, maintaining a rigid asset allocation might lead to missed opportunities or heightened risk during market downturns.

For instance, during periods of economic expansion, equities tend to perform well as businesses grow and consumer spending increases. In contrast, during economic downturns, assets like gold or bonds might perform better, preserving wealth and providing stability. By dynamically adjusting allocations in response to these conditions, investors can maintain a portfolio that aligns with current market realities, achieving both growth and stability.

Adjusting Equities Based on Economic Cycles

Equities generally perform well during economic upswings when corporate earnings and consumer spending are on the rise. In such times, a higher equity allocation can capture growth opportunities, especially in sectors poised to benefit from economic trends, such as technology, finance, and consumer goods. For Indian investors, a greater focus on equities during growth periods allows them to capitalize on India's expanding economy, which is projected to grow steadily over the coming years.

Conversely, during economic slowdowns or high-volatility periods, reducing exposure to equities can minimize risk. By reallocating some funds from equities to more stable assets, investors can protect their portfolios from potential market downturns, reducing losses while awaiting economic recovery.

Gold as a Counterbalance During Uncertain Times

Gold has long been valued for its counter-cyclical properties, making it an ideal asset during periods of economic uncertainty or inflation. When inflation rises, gold prices often increase as investors seek to preserve purchasing power. Similarly, during periods of currency depreciation or geopolitical instability, gold serves as a safe-haven asset, providing stability when other investments may falter.

For a dynamically managed portfolio, increasing the gold allocation during uncertain periods or when inflation is high can help protect wealth and maintain purchasing power. As India's economy is influenced by both local and global economic factors, Indian investors may find gold especially valuable during periods of currency volatility and external shocks that could impact the rupee's value.

Fixed Income as a Stabilizer in High-Interest-Rate Environments

Fixed-income investments, such as government bonds, corporate bonds, and fixed deposits, play a crucial role in stabilizing a portfolio. During periods of rising interest rates, fixed-income investments can provide steady returns and reduce portfolio volatility. Indian investors, particularly those nearing retirement or with low-risk tolerance, may consider increasing their allocation to bonds when interest rates are on the rise.

Dynamic asset allocation allows for adjustments based on the prevailing interest rate environment. For instance, as the Reserve Bank of India (RBI) raises rates to combat inflation, bond yields may increase, making fixed-income assets more attractive relative to equities. Allocating a portion of the portfolio to bonds during such periods enhances income predictability and capital protection.

Utilizing Alternative Investments for Enhanced Diversification

Alternative investments, such as real estate, REITs, and infrastructure funds, offer diversification beyond traditional asset classes, providing additional layers of stability. For instance, real estate and infrastructure investments are relatively uncorrelated with the stock market, making them effective during periods of high equity market volatility. Real estate investment trusts (REITs) in India, supported by the government's focus on infrastructure, provide income through rental yields and potential capital appreciation.

By allocating a portion of their portfolio to alternatives in high-volatility environments, investors can smoothen returns, reduce portfolio risk, and hedge against equity downturns. Dynamic allocation enables investors to adjust exposure to alternatives based on real estate market cycles, government policies, and infrastructure growth.

Role of Technology in Dynamic Asset Allocation

Advancements in technology have made dynamic asset allocation more accessible and efficient for retail investors. Robo-advisors, algorithmic trading, and financial platforms enable investors to set automated rebalancing strategies based on predefined conditions or economic indicators. Platforms like Zerodha, Groww, and Upstox allow investors to make timely adjustments with minimal friction, helping them align their portfolios with changing economic conditions.

Robo-advisors, for example, monitor market data and recommend rebalancing based on individual goals and risk tolerance. This automation enhances decision-making, allowing for more disciplined and responsive adjustments to portfolio allocations without requiring manual intervention.

Implementing a Systematic Approach to Dynamic Rebalancing

Dynamic asset allocation requires a structured approach to rebalancing, allowing investors to adjust their portfolios without overreacting to short-term market fluctuations. Setting a predefined schedule for portfolio review, such as quarterly or bi-annually, allows for regular adjustments while avoiding unnecessary trading. Investors can also establish specific thresholds—such as a 10% deviation in asset allocation—to trigger rebalancing when markets experience significant shifts.

Additionally, staying informed on key economic indicators, such as GDP growth, inflation rates, and central bank policies, allows investors to make timely decisions about portfolio allocation. For example, increasing exposure to equities during high-growth periods, or adding more to gold during inflationary cycles, ensures that the portfolio remains aligned with prevailing economic trends.

A Dynamic Path to Long-Term Success

Dynamic asset allocation enables Indian investors to build portfolios that are both resilient and growth-oriented, adapting to market conditions with a proactive strategy. By adjusting allocations based on economic cycles, inflation trends, interest rate environments, and asset performance, investors can mitigate risks, capitalize on opportunities, and achieve long-term financial goals. For Indian investors navigating a rapidly evolving economy, dynamic asset allocation offers a robust framework that balances wealth creation with wealth preservation.

Building Wealth in an Uncertain Economic Landscape

Building wealth in an uncertain economic landscape requires a strategic approach that prioritizes resilience, adaptability, and informed decision-making. Economic uncertainty—driven by factors such as inflation, market volatility, geopolitical tensions, and unpredictable policy changes—poses unique challenges to investors, necessitating a thoughtful allocation of assets that can withstand fluctuations and deliver consistent growth. In such a landscape, investors benefit from a diversified portfolio that blends high-growth assets, like equities, with stable, wealth-preserving assets, such as gold and fixed income. This mix not only captures growth during favorable market periods but also provides a buffer against downturns, offering protection and stability.

One of the core principles in wealth-building during uncertain times is diversification. By spreading investments across various asset classes and sectors, investors can mitigate the impact of any single asset or market segment underperforming. Equities remain a vital part of a growth-focused portfolio, particularly in high-growth sectors like technology, healthcare, and renewable energy, which align with long-term economic trends. However, given the risks associated with stock market volatility, including some defensive assets—such as bonds and gold—enhances portfolio stability. Bonds provide predictable income and reduce overall volatility, while gold acts as a hedge against inflation and currency depreciation, particularly valuable during economic downturns.

Flexibility and adaptability are equally important for wealth-building in uncertain environments. Dynamic asset allocation, where investors adjust their portfolio based on changing market conditions and economic indicators, allows for a proactive response to emerging risks and opportunities. For instance, during inflationary periods, increasing allocation to inflation-protected assets like gold can preserve purchasing power, while during economic recoveries, a higher allocation to equities can capture growth. Advances in technology, including robo-advisors and algorithmic trading, have made dynamic allocation accessible to retail investors, enabling timely portfolio adjustments based on real-time market data.

Additionally, a disciplined investment approach, such as investing through systematic investment plans (SIPs), can be highly effective. SIPs encourage consistent contributions, allowing investors to average out the purchase cost and benefit from compounding over time. This strategy is particularly advantageous in volatile markets, as it reduces the need to time investments, enabling wealth accumulation despite market fluctuations.

Finally, staying informed and educated about economic trends, policy changes, and market developments is essential for making sound financial decisions. In an uncertain landscape, knowledge is a powerful tool that empowers investors to identify opportunities, avoid pitfalls, and make adjustments as necessary. By combining diversification, flexibility, and a disciplined approach, investors can build wealth that is resilient to economic uncertainties. This strategic framework not only preserves capital but also fosters sustainable growth, allowing investors to thrive in both stable and volatile economic conditions.

Conclusion

Key Takeaways

Balancing Growth and Stability through Diversification
A well-diversified portfolio is essential for building wealth in uncertain economic conditions. Combining high-growth assets, like equities, with wealth-preserving assets, such as gold and fixed income, enhances resilience. Equities drive capital appreciation, while defensive assets provide a buffer against market downturns, stabilizing the portfolio across economic cycles.

Gold as a Hedge Against Uncertainty
Gold remains a crucial asset in the face of inflation, currency depreciation, and geopolitical risks. As a stable, counter-cyclical asset, gold provides a safe-hold when other assets underperform, making it especially valuable during economic volatility. Digital gold investments have made gold more accessible, allowing investors to add it seamlessly to their portfolios for added security.

Dynamic Asset Allocation: Adapting to Market Shifts
Dynamic asset allocation allows investors to adjust their portfolios based on changing economic conditions. By increasing or decreasing exposure to equities, gold, and fixed income as the economy evolves, investors can capture growth opportunities while managing risk. Technological advancements, including robo-advisors and algorithmic trading, now make dynamic allocation more

accessible to retail investors, enabling proactive portfolio adjustments.

Harnessing Technology for Informed Investment Decisions

Technology plays a vital role in enhancing investment accessibility, transparency, and efficiency. Platforms offering robo-advisory services, digital gold, and online trading have democratized investing, allowing individuals to make informed, data-driven decisions. These tools enable investors to automate strategies, access financial insights, and execute real-time adjustments, all of which support better long-term outcomes.

Systematic Investment Plans (SIPs) for Consistent Wealth Building

SIPs provide a disciplined approach to investing, especially valuable in volatile markets. By investing regularly, investors benefit from cost averaging and compounding, gradually building wealth without needing to time the market. SIPs are effective for accumulating assets over the long term, making them a foundational strategy for many Indian investors.

Central Bank and Institutional Demand for Gold

The consistent accumulation of gold by central banks, particularly in emerging markets, underscores its enduring value. As a hedge against currency volatility and a reliable store of value, gold plays a strategic role in both national reserves and individual portfolios, signaling confidence in its protective qualities.

Long-Term Outlook for Indian Equities
Indian equities remain a critical component of growth-oriented portfolios, benefiting from India's economic expansion and high-growth sectors. However, investors should balance this growth with caution, as inflation, interest rate changes, and global economic influences can impact stock performance. Strategic sectoral diversification across technology, finance, and consumer goods further enhances growth potential.

Building Wealth in Uncertain Times
A balanced approach that integrates flexibility, diversification, and disciplined investing is key to building wealth amidst uncertainty. By maintaining a blend of growth and defensive assets, adapting allocations in response to market shifts, and staying informed about economic trends, investors can achieve both resilience and growth. This holistic strategy provides a foundation for long-term financial security, enabling investors to thrive regardless of market conditions.

Strategic Insights for the Indian Investor

Strategic insights for Indian investors revolve around adapting to a dynamic economic landscape with a well-balanced, diversified portfolio that captures growth opportunities while managing risk. In a rapidly developing economy like India's, equities offer substantial potential for wealth creation, especially in high-growth sectors such as technology, finance, and consumer goods. However, given the volatility inherent in stock markets and the potential for global economic shifts to impact India, investors should balance their portfolios with stable assets like gold and fixed income. Gold serves as a hedge against inflation and currency fluctuations, providing protection in uncertain times, while fixed-income investments offer steady returns and reduce portfolio volatility, making them particularly valuable for risk-averse or retirement-focused investors.

To further optimize their portfolios, Indian investors can leverage dynamic asset allocation, adjusting their exposure to equities, gold, and bonds based on prevailing market conditions and economic indicators. This flexible approach allows investors to capitalize on growth during expansions and shift towards defensive assets in downturns. Technological advancements have made this strategy more accessible, with platforms offering robo-advisors and algorithmic trading tools that facilitate real-time adjustments and data-driven decision-making. Additionally, systematic investment plans (SIPs) provide a disciplined path to long-term wealth accumulation, particularly for younger or first-time investors. By consistently investing a fixed amount, SIPs allow investors to build wealth gradually, taking advantage of cost averaging and compounding without the need to time the market.

Moreover, the growing emphasis on sustainability has made Environmental, Social, and Governance (ESG) considerations an essential part of modern investment strategy. Investors are increasingly focusing on companies with responsible practices, aligning their portfolios with long-term environmental and ethical goals. Finally, staying informed about economic policies, central bank actions, and global events is crucial for making proactive adjustments to a portfolio. By combining diversification, flexibility, and financial literacy, Indian investors can build resilient portfolios that navigate uncertainty while capturing India's economic potential. This strategic approach provides a foundation for long-term financial security, enabling investors to pursue growth while safeguarding their wealth against volatility.

Final Thoughts on the Future of Gold and the Stock Market

As we look toward the future, gold and the stock market will continue to play essential, yet distinct, roles in the financial landscape. Gold, with its centuries-old reputation as a store of value, remains a powerful hedge against inflation, currency fluctuations, and global instability. In an increasingly uncertain world marked by economic shifts, geopolitical tensions, and evolving monetary policies, gold's role as a stabilizer in portfolios becomes even more pronounced. Digital gold investments have further broadened access, enabling a new generation of investors to incorporate gold into their wealth-building strategies, solidifying its place in modern finance.

The stock market, on the other hand, offers unparalleled opportunities for growth and wealth creation. For Indian investors, the rapid expansion of sectors like technology, finance, and infrastructure positions Indian equities as a promising avenue for capital appreciation. Yet, the stock market's inherent volatility and sensitivity to both domestic and global economic shifts underscore the importance of diversification. While equities provide growth potential, they are susceptible to economic cycles, making it essential for investors to balance this risk with defensive assets like gold.

The intersection of technology and investing has transformed how investors engage with both gold and stocks. Technological innovations such as robo-advisors, algorithmic trading, and blockchain-backed digital gold have made investing more accessible, efficient, and transparent. These tools empower investors to make data-driven decisions and adjust their portfolios dynamically in response to market conditions, creating a more agile investment strategy. For Indian investors, embracing these advancements and integrating both traditional and digital assets can create a resilient portfolio that adapts to the complexities of an evolving economy.

In the coming years, the complementary nature of gold and equities will continue to support balanced, diversified portfolios. Gold's enduring stability provides a buffer against volatility, while equities drive capital growth, allowing investors to capture the best of both worlds. By staying informed, adopting a flexible approach, and leveraging technology, investors can navigate future uncertainties with confidence. In an era of rapid change, the strategic combination of gold and stocks offers a foundation for long-term financial security and growth, ensuring that portfolios remain robust and prosperous regardless of economic conditions.

Appendices

Glossary of Key Terms

Asset Allocation

The process of distributing investments across different asset classes, such as equities, bonds, and gold, to balance risk and reward in alignment with an investor's goals, time horizon, and risk tolerance.

Bull Market

A period in which stock prices are generally rising, often driven by economic growth, high investor confidence, and increased spending.

Central Bank

The principal monetary authority in a country, such as the Reserve Bank of India (RBI), responsible for managing currency stability, controlling inflation, and regulating financial institutions.

Commodities

Raw materials or primary agricultural products, such as gold, oil, and wheat, that are traded on financial markets. Commodities often serve as hedges against inflation.

Currency Depreciation

The decline in a currency's value relative to another currency, reducing purchasing power and affecting the cost of imported goods. Currency depreciation can make gold more attractive as a store of value.

Diversification

A risk management strategy that involves spreading investments across various asset classes, sectors, or geographies to reduce overall risk in a portfolio.

Dynamic Asset Allocation

An investment strategy that involves regularly adjusting the mix of assets in a portfolio based on changes in market conditions, economic indicators, and an investor's financial goals.

Environmental, Social, and Governance (ESG)

A set of criteria used to evaluate a company's commitment to sustainable and ethical practices in areas such as environmental conservation, social responsibility, and corporate governance.

Equities

Securities that represent ownership in a company, commonly known as stocks. Equities offer the potential for capital appreciation and, in some cases, dividend income.

Fixed Income

Investments, such as bonds or fixed deposits, that provide regular income through fixed interest payments. Fixed income assets are generally more stable and are used to reduce volatility in a portfolio.

Geopolitical Risk

The potential impact of international political and economic events, such as wars or trade disputes, on financial markets. Geopolitical risk often increases demand for safe-haven assets like gold.

Gold ETF (Exchange-Traded Fund)

A type of ETF that tracks the price of gold, allowing investors to gain exposure to gold without physically holding it. Gold ETFs are traded on stock exchanges like shares.

Hedge

An investment strategy used to reduce risk by offsetting potential losses in one asset with gains in another. Gold is often used as a hedge against inflation and market volatility.

Inflation

The rate at which the general level of prices for goods and services rises, eroding purchasing power. Gold is commonly viewed as a hedge against inflation.

Interest Rate

The cost of borrowing money, typically set by a central bank. Interest rates influence investment returns, consumer spending, and economic growth, affecting both the stock and bond markets.

Market Volatility

The degree of variation in asset prices over a given period. High volatility means larger fluctuations in price, while low volatility indicates stable price movements.

Portfolio Rebalancing

The process of realigning the weightings of assets in a portfolio to maintain a target allocation, typically done periodically to reflect changes in market conditions or investment goals.

Robo-Advisor

An automated platform that provides investment advice and portfolio management services using algorithms, often at lower costs than traditional financial advisors.

Safe-Hold Asset

An asset that retains or increases in value during periods of economic uncertainty. Gold is commonly viewed as a safe-hold asset due to its stability during market downturns.

Systematic Investment Plan (SIP)

An investment method in which a fixed amount is regularly invested in a mutual fund or other financial asset. SIPs are commonly used in India to build wealth over time through regular contributions.

Tokenization

The process of converting real-world assets, such as stocks or gold, into digital tokens on a blockchain, making them easily transferable and enhancing transparency.

Yield

The income earned from an investment, typically expressed as an annual percentage of the asset's cost or market price. Yield is a key metric for evaluating fixed-income investments.

References

1. **International Monetary Fund.** (2024). *World economic outlook.* Retrieved from https://www.imf.org
2. **Reserve Bank of India.** (2024). *Annual report.* Retrieved from https://www.rbi.org.in
3. **National Securities Depository Limited.** (2023). *Growth in retail investor participation and digital trading.* Retrieved from https://www.nsdl.co.in
4. **National Infrastructure Pipeline.** (2024). *Government initiatives in India's infrastructure development.* Retrieved from https://www.investindia.gov.in
5. **World Gold Council.** (2023). *Gold as an investment in emerging markets.* Retrieved from https://www.gold.org
6. **MMTC-PAMP.** (2023). *Digital gold platform features and benefits.* Retrieved from https://www.mmtcpamp.com
7. **Goldman Sachs.** (2024). *Gold price outlook and inflationary trends.* Retrieved from https://www.goldmansachs.com
8. **Bombay Stock Exchange.** (2022). *Historical performance of the Sensex.* Retrieved from https://www.bseindia.com
9. **Think Fish.** (2024). *10 investment trends to watch in 2024.* Retrieved from https://thinkfish.co
10. **Capgemini.** (2024). *Investment trends 2024.* Retrieved from https://www.capgemini.com
11. **McKinsey & Company.** (2023). *A look at the technology trends that matter most.* Retrieved from https://www.mckinsey.com
12. **Deloitte.** (2023). *Technology industry outlook.* Retrieved from https://www.deloitte.com/cbc/en/Industries/

REFERENCES

tmt/analysis/technology-industry-outlook.html

13. **World Gold Council.** (2021). *Gold demand trends.* Retrieved from https://www.gold.org
14. **Reuters.** (2024). *Gold nears record highs amid geopolitical uncertainties.* Retrieved from https://www.reuters.com
15. **Business Standard.** (2024). *IMF retains India's growth forecast at 7% for FY25.* Retrieved from https://www.business-standard.com
16. **Oliver Wyman.** (2024). *Asset management trends for 2024.* Retrieved from https://www.oliverwyman.com
17. **Zerodha Varsity.** (2024). *Investment education and market analysis.* Retrieved from https://www.zerodha.com
18. **National Stock Exchange of India.** (2020). *NSE market analysis and economic growth.* Retrieved from https://www.nseindia.com
19. **KPMG.** (2024). *Emerging trends in infrastructure investment.* Retrieved from https://kpmg.com
20. **Times of Money.** (2023). *How technology is changing gold investing.* Retrieved from https://www.timesofmoney.com
21. **Reuters.** (2024). *RBI rate cut outlook amid inflation trends.* Retrieved from https://www.reuters.com
22. **World Economic Forum.** (2023). *Blockchain and tokenization in modern finance.* Retrieved from https://www.weforum.org
23. **Business Insider Markets.** (2024). *Gold price forecast and market trends.* Retrieved from https://markets.businessinsider.com

Milton Keynes UK
Ingram Content Group UK Ltd.
UKHW022235201124
451458UK00004B/24